MEANING IN SUFFERING
COMFORT IN CRISIS
THROUGH LOGOTHERAPY

MEANING IN SUFFERING
COMFORT IN CRISIS
THROUGH LOGOTHERAPY

Elisabeth Lukas

TRANSLATED FROM THE GERMAN BY JOSEPH B. FABRY

INSTITUTE OF LOGOTHERAPY PRESS
Berkeley, California

The Southern German Institute for Logotherapy (Dr. Elisabeth Lukas, Director) has its office at Geschwister Scholl Platz 8, D-8080, Furstenfeldbruck, (Munich), West Germany. Telephone 08 141/1 80 41.

Institute of Logotherapy Press
2000 Dwight Way
Berkeley, California 94704

Translated from the German (Auch dein leiden hat sinn) by Joseph B. Fabry

Cover design by Jose Barbosa

Wordprocessed by Pauline McGuire

Typesetting by Cragmont/ExPress

Printing by Edwards Brothers, Inc., Ann Arbor, Michigan

Manufactured in the United States of America

Library of Congress Cataloging-in-Publication Data:
Lukas, Elisabeth S.
    Meaning in suffering.

    Translation of: Auch dein Leiden hat Sinn.
    Bibliography: p.
    1. Logotherapy. 2. Suffering. I. Title.
RC489.L6L8313 1986b   616.89'14   86-3003
ISBN 0-917867-05-X (pbk.)

SPONSORS

Anonymous
Lawrence Au, D.Min.
Margaret Marx Davis-Finck
Mignon Eisenberg, Ph.D.
Judith Fabry
Willis Cornell Finck
Sunny Fox
Robin Goodenough, Ph.D., J.D.
William B. Gould, Ph.D.
Stephen Kalmar, Ph.D.
Robert C. Leslie, Ph.D.
Vera J. Lieban Kalmar. Ed.D.
Velma Schwise Marx
Patricia M. Murphy

Thanks are due to Hyman Roudman for editing, Judith Fabry for typing the manuscript, and Hyman Roudman, Andy Kincart, and Katherine Lieban for paste-up.

Contents

FOREWORD

My first experience in searching for meaning occurred when I was three years old, long before logotherapy was developed. It happened early one morning in a brown shingled house on Pine Avenue in Berkeley, California, where I lived at the time. The day was Christmas and the air was full of excitement.

As a gift I received an heirloom doll which belonged to my mother as a child. It was about two feet tall, with a beautiful porcelain head and long hair, jointed arms and legs, an old fashioned embroidered dress, and black patent leather one-button shoes. I promptly named her Marilyn. She was a grown-up doll instead of a baby doll and I felt very grown up to be trusted with it.

My other gift was a doll-sized wicker basket filled with doll clothes pins so that when I washed her clothes I could also hang them up. These two gifts were very meaningful to me and seemed to represent love and trust.

However, the meaning changed somewhat when my brother, who was four years older, chased me around the room in some kind of game, slipped on the waxed floor, and fell against the low wooden chest on which Marilyn rested. Crash, she fell to the floor, her head broken! Crash went my heart, broken into as many pieces as my new doll.

Even at that age I knew there was absolutely no money available to buy a new head. That was the reality. No one was scolded for the accident; perhaps everyone was sad.

And so I pondered hour after hour, "What does it mean to have a doll with no head especially when it hurts so much?" I did not know the grown-up word "suffering" but I did understand "hurt" so I decided to love her regardless of her condition.

Since that time many years ago I have often made similar choices and looked for meaning in what might appear to be a meaningless situation. Like you, I have known joy in positive experiences of love, truth, and beauty. Like you, I have known pleasure in my own or in other people's accomplishments. And probably also like you, I have found meaning in the midst of pain, grief, and despair. So too, like a doll with a broken head, I have needed to be loved and that too has happened.

And so it goes. At any moment in a person's life the expected routine or anticipated success may seem important or may suddenly be without personal meaning. The challenging dragon may rear its head, flash its eyes, spit fire and roar, "I dare you to find meaning in this."

The person with courage accepts the dare, makes decisions, and acts on the basis of decisions. Acting with courage is not based on feeling confident. The courageous person may instead feel a bone-wrenching fear, yet in spite of it does not submit to the internal tyranny of overpowering negative feelings. Many people become so accustomed to negative thinking that choosing to change their attitudes is not easy. Yet it is possible in spite of limited knowledge, insufficient evidence, family background, physical or psychological disabilities or current problems. Change often requires courageous action and the willingness, as Frankl put it, "to face your fate without flinching." Sometimes this requires acting "as if," acting as if feeling strong and confident when in fact feeling weak and inadequate.

This is one of the basic tenets of logotherapy—that a person has feelings, the feelings do not need to "have" and control a person. It is one of the issues of Elisabeth Lukas' book, *Meaning in Suffering*, a book that demonstrates how a phychotherapist can help others take charge of their own lives with what Viktor Frankl has called "the defiant power of the human spirit." When this power is released, people can find meaning in any situation, even in situations of inevitable suffering .

To find meaning is to find validation. The care and humaneness that Dr. Lukas demonstrates to her patients is a validating rarity in these days when many therapists limit themselves to the traditional 50 minute hour and sometimes seem unconcerned about the agony that can be experienced by the patients between sessions. In case study after case study the author of *Meaning in Suffering* reveals her psychological knowledge, her skillful and creative use of logotherapy, and her concern for other people. She is not biased against being involved with them. Yet she carefully monitors her involvement so as not to contribute to the development of iatrogenic problems (damage caused by therapists saying or doing the wrong things or not saying and doing what needs to be done). Iatrogenic problems are possible when a therapist loses perspective, becomes overly involved, or perhaps reinforces the clients' negative reinforcing prophesies and invites further "sickness" instead of health.

The subject of iatrogenic problems is an important part of the book and, in my opinion, needs more study by those who intend to be, or who already are, mental health professionals. Also valuable are the suggestions about how to use logotherapy in specific ways with people who have neurotic-type personalities as well as with those suffering with some form of psychosis. For example, learning how to laugh at symptoms, even exaggerating them, is a logotherapeutic technique called "paradoxical intention." Laughter works because people do not fear what they find to be amusing.

In addition to paradoxical intention, the other major methods that Dr. Lukas focuses upon are dereflection and modulation of attitudes. When clients are encouraged to search for meaning in every area of life, their attitudes are changed in important ways. Especially interesting is the concept of a dereflection group. In this, group members are instructed to talk only about the positive aspects of their lives, positive things they observe, or negative problems they have overcome in positive ways. This positive view may be new to those who continually focus only on negatives or past history. Her almost allergic reaction to "working through" is well worth considering.

At the present time logotherapy, like other therapeutic modalities is often used to supplement other systems. For example, I frequently use logotherapy in conjunction with transactional analysis and gestalt therapy in my private practice. In transactional analysis terms, Elisabeth Lukas in *Meaning in Suffering* reflects her caring Parent as well as her empathic Child and knowledgeable Adult. This book will inevitably encourage and direct psychotherapists and counselors who recognize the need and potential people have to transcend themselves and move beyond egocentricity. The book is also useful in courses which compare various therapeutic theories and modalities

CHAPTER ONE

Comfort Where
No Cure Is Possible

For thousands of years people have done pretty well without the science of psychotherapy. Yet, something like psychotherapy has always existed—through persons who, with charisma, persuasiveness, and force of conviction, were able to bring comfort to those looking for help. Such help was usually based on a specific philosophy of life.

The afflicted were promised eternal wellbeing and justice in the hereafter, or their suffering was presented as a test on their way to happiness, or suggestive powers were used to exorcise the evil, or philosophic-ethical images were invoked to make blows of fate bearable. Psychotherapy was religion and vice versa.

This embeddedness in mysticism made it difficult for psychotherapy to find a scientific approach. Today, if we try to find rational explanations for irrational behavior, and offer rational help for irrational psychological problems, we stand on an extremely narrow ridge between two abysses: on the one side lies the danger of reverting to mysticism, and on the other side the danger of slipping into a mechanized manipulation of the human person.

Has psychology, on its long development through magic, exorcism, trickery, demagoguery, occultism, and fanaticism, finally attained the status of science? In recent decades great strides were made in that direction. Successes were conspicuous and resulted in a great variety of tools in a giant psychological workshop to serve humans but unfortunately the specifically human dimension—the spirit—was left out. "Psychotherapy without magic" has been replaced by "psychotherapy without spirit." What was gained in the field of science was lost from humanity. Psychotherapists may choose from a great number of methods but are forced to walk on that narrow ridge between old views and new perspectives, between speculative interpretations and human programming. It is a path illuminated by alarmingly few firm criteria.

This book is written for those who trust psychotherapy to find comfort. The trust of the patients is valuable but must not be blindly given, or they may be pushed into one of the abysses left or right. They may fall under the spell of speculative hypotheses from which they cannot free themselves, or they may be wrecked by a cold, impersonal conditioning process because they no longer can sense the meanings of their lives.

The book is also for psychotherapists who walk that narrow ridge, weighted down by responsibility for those who trust them. Few are the guideposts, many the contradictory theories, the confusion, the criticism. What school are they to believe, what concepts to make their own?

This book suggests a path for the lay reader as well as for the professional, a path through the maze of psychological schools to a psychotherapy which no longer is a myth and includes the human spirit, combines science and humanity, and thus justifies our trust, especially the trust of the *suffering person*. The value of a psychotherapy is tested by what it can do for those who suffer and need comfort. Where help no longer is possible, comfort must be given; where no comfort is possible, any psychotherapy is useless.

OLD VIEWS

Early psychotherapy was not concerned with comfort. Its central concern was to uncover human motivations, unmask hidden drives and unconscious emotions, and reveal secret intentions. From the very beginning, depth psychologists made it their business to search out, find, and explain negative aspects. They were looking for human weaknesses, libidinous dreams and symbols from which they could draw conclusions. Thus, psychotherapy began from a negative basis. Positive aspects were of little interest, of no use in practice, and suspected of masking something negative. Often the positive was denied, ideals and ethical values were interpreted as "mere sublimation of primitive drives," love, faith, loyalty, or conscience were denied. Why worry about the noble, helpful, and good if in reality people are ruled by sexual desires and aggressions, every "noble motivation" only the mask of another, deeper and "ignoble motivation"? This was the era of cynicism, nihilism, atheism. Philosophers discovered the meaninglessness of human existence, artists were encouraged to create works of the "unesthetic." The human being as the age-long image of God was unmasked to show egocentricity and lust for gratification. Where, in this approach, was comfort possible for suffering people?

Even the non-suffering, the normal, the healthy were deprived of a solid base by confronting them with their "hidden aspects", the dark depths of their instinctual nature.

This picture of human nature left little room for free, rational decisions. The person was seen as a battlefield of three rather mystical forces: id, ego, and superego. Id symbolized the primitive drives, especially sex and aggression; the superego symbolized the 'father image," or the totality of societal forces, as a controlling court. Between warring id and superego stood the ego, facing reality, making concessions to them.

What is questionable in this picture is our proclaimed powerlessness against our own weaknesses, our total dependence on the all-determining force of our drives.

If, for example, a patient mentions that once, while playing with her doll, she broke off its arm and this made her sad, the episode could be interpreted as follows: because of oedipal conflicts, she subconsciously hated her mother, wanted all her father's love and did not want to share it with her mother. She repressed her hate, the doll became a symbol for her mother, an acceptable outlet for her accumulated aggression. Her id urged her to express her hate, her superego prevented her from actually attacking her mother, so the symbolic act of "destroy-ing the doll" remained the only way out. When she broke the arm of the doll she unconsciously wanted to break the neck of her mother. Such interpretations are dangerous and bring little comfort to the patient. Childhood pain about the broken doll, which may have lost its importance long ago, becomes now an infantile act of vengeance against the mother, which makes the daughter shudder even as an adult woman.

For a long time psychotherapists paid little attention to the effects of their actions. They were certain that uncovering causes would make symptoms vanish. Psychoanalysis, of course, has developed and many practitioners are cautious about diagnoses, and do consider the feelings of patients. But the basic concept remains. Therapy still deals with uncovering and unmasking, and this means a devaluation of ideals. But values and ideals are precisely what provides support even in severe suffering. Early psychoanalysis not only did not give comfort to the suffering but robbed them of values which might have brought comfort.

In my student days I came across a vivid example of this reductionist thinking that suspects a "hidden" in everything and devaluates everything, down to the roots of human existence. It was an experiment to compare the strength of various drives in rats.

Rats were shown various objects from which they were separated by an electrically charged wire net. First, a sexually deprived rat faced a rat of the opposite sex. The rat immediately crossed the net to meet its partner. When put back to her original place she did not try it a second time. The sex partner did not tempt her to experience the electric shock a second time.

In a second experiment a starved rat was facing food. The rat crossed the wire a few times but gave up as soon as its worst hunger was stilled.

In a third experiment a rat mother faced one of her young, separated by the electric net. The rat kept running to her young, regardless how often she was put back, until she was dead. From these experiments it was concluded that the mother instinct was stronger than self-preservation, and this again stronger than the sex drive.

So far so good. But some depth psychologists drew conclusions according to their own concept of human nature. "Ah," they said, "what human parents do for their children also is done not out of selflessness and love, but to gratify their own strongest drive, the maternal instinct. All sacrifices of a mother are made because of the pleasure she gains by gratifying her strongest instinct." Mother love reduced to the simple gratification of a drive!

Viktor Frankl, one of the most prominent critics of reductionism, admits that unmasking has its legitimate place in psychotherapy, but adds:

"Unmasking, or debunking, however, should stop as soon as

one is confronted with what is authentic and genuine in man; e.g., man's desire for a life that is as meaningful as possible. If it does not stop then, the man who does the debunking merely betrays his own will to depreciate the spiritual aspirations of another."

This, then, is one abyss which threatens psychotherapists in their wanderings on the ridge; a relapse into devaluation stemming from the early days of psychoanalysis. Those who deal with suffering must not increase suffering, just to discover "truths," such as speculations about id, ego, and superego, and their internecine struggles. If we see people as determined by their drives, torn between gratification and non-gratification from childhood on, we cannot help or comfort. As Frankl says, we can only devaluate and destroy until the genuinely human is eliminated and what remains as psychological concept is at best the outline of a rat.

Depth psychologists are not alone in misrepresenting human nature. Rats are the pet animals of behaviorists whose aim is to be strictly scientific, not accepting anything that is not clearly proved. After the period of unmasking and devaluating came the time of rationality. A rational society wants rational propositions: the time had come to bury mysticism in psychotherapy once and for all.

In behaviorism human beings are no longer battlegrounds for inner forces. Since nobody can look into the human psyche, it was declared "empty," like the famous "black box,"—no one knows what is in it. This was the time when "spirit" disappeared from psychology: for thousands of years spirit was considered something more than a visible and explorable organ; now, according to scientific principles, it was empty.

There was one ray of hope. The basis of what we can know about human nature was no longer purely negative; negative and positive aspects were equally considered, as "stimuli" for the black box. The original model was simple. The human being was a machine that digested data: on one side entered stimuli from the environment and perhaps also from one's own body; from the other side behavior reactions went out. What happened in between was at first not known. Today's behaviorists have worked out an incredibly complex system of criss-crossing currents between stimuli and reactions so the "black box" is no longer regarded as empty but as a giant computer—which has not made it more human. The rat outline has been superseded by electronic wire mesh, where positive and negative reinforcers are linked with conditioned and unconditioned stimuli, which again can be unlinked so human behavior is totally manipulable. As a matter of fact, behavior thinking was born at a time when the first computer and robot models came into use: the parallels are obvious.

Can the psychological concepts of behaviorism give comfort to the sufferer? A computer can be repaired and reprogrammed but can it be comforted? This sounds ridiculous because computers need no comforting. But what about human beings seen as computers? Do they, too, need no comforting?

This is the dilemma of a psychology without spirit: To be consistent all behavior must be sufficiently measurable, even joy, hope, sorrow, and suffering. To evade this dilemma, human phenomena are declared problems beyond the field of competence for those schools of psychology. Behavior therapy has remained a treatment technology, in spite of many modern and positive attempts to broaden it on the human plane. Comforting the sufferer is not part of its task. It concentrates on what can be treated, and its "strategy" is always to intervene in existing stimulus-reaction links, turn off old currents, and turn on new ones.

An example are the antabuse therapies. Drinks of alcoholics are "spiced" with something that causes nausea. Every time they drink they get sick. If this is done for a long enough time, this technique is successful because—at least for a while—those treated avoid alcohol. The conditioning—alcohol equals feeling good—is gradually replaced by another—alcohol equals feeling bad. The software is changed, a new program is initiated. Unsolved remain such questions as why people started drinking, how they feel about themselves as alcoholics, and—most importantly—how can they live from here on as "cured" alcoholics.

Behavior therapy cannot offer strategies where it cannot bring about behavioral changes through manipulating stimuli. Their term "strategy" indicates the limitation. There are no such things as "strategic compassion" or "strategic comfort". Where patients face unavoidable suffering, they need neither unmasking nor manipulation. They need psychotherapists who can meet them as a "thou."

Thus, behaviorist thinking also may lead into an abyss—seeing the human as a machine—unless the therapist realizes the limitations of behaviorist techniques. Many of these techniques are effective and useful but help only in small areas while large regions of the personality remain untouched. As long as psychotherapists realize this, they can apply behavior therapy without losing their footing on the narrow ridge. But they have to be aware of its limitations.

NEW PERSPECTIVES

Both psychoanalysis and behavior therapy are based on determinism: human beings are seen as determined by inner or outer influences, genetic or environmental conditions, and intended or incidental factors, all scientifically proved. Every psychology student knows about the importance of heredity, environment, early childhood and sociological influences, it being understood that these scientifically verifiable influences decisively pre- and co-determine our lives and behavior. A reading of the literature on influences during pregnancy, for instance, may give the impression that "all is fixed" before life has even begun.

Extremes create their own limitations. The determinism that has dominated psychological thinking for more than half a century, is being questioned. Foremost among those questioning is the Viennese psychiatrist Viktor E. Frankl who goes beyond depth psychology and behaviorism. He considers the dimension of the human spirit, beyond all psychophysical and psychological interactions. *The human spirit, by definition, is the dimension of human freedom and therefore not subject to deterministic laws.*

Freedom is a word often misused. To avoid misunderstandings, Frankl does not speak of freedom *from* something, especially not from conditions (no one is free from his or her physical and psychological conditions). Frankl speaks of freedom *to* something—a freely taken attitude toward these conditions. He stresses the attitude of "despite," our choice of response to fate.

Here a basis is provided to comfort and help people, regardless how inescapable the suffering. Only by overcoming determinism is comforting possible; this is done by acknowledging the dimension of the human spirit.

Frankl is convinced that human beings are never completely helpless victims of fate. He defines "fate" as what lies beyond human freedom—beyond our power and responsibility. Fate is the totality of all determining factors. But it is also the springboard of our freedom—the challenge to respond to fate (in contrast to animals) *in various ways,* and (again in contrast to animals) to be response-able for our choices. Fate, for Frankl, is not the cause of human thoughts and actions but their precondition. It does not explain our reactions but triggers them. Fate makes us human because it forces us to choose among the available potentialities, and thus to make use of our human freedom.

The clear distinction between fate and freedom is basic to Frankl's logotherapy and plays a major part in logotherapeutic counseling. Many problems can be alleviated by directing the patients' attention to areas of freedom, where they still have the opportunity to come to terms with fate, to direct attention away from unchangeable situations and their possible causes or consequences. To fight fate where there is no way out leads to despair.

Case No. 1

A young man, in great embarrassment, confessed to me his feeling of guilt because he felt sexually aroused when physical therapy treatments were applied by women. His guilt feelings could be quickly eliminated, without long explanations of repressed sexual desires or complexes. Two things were made clear to him: First, his body reactions were purely biological and neurophysiological, and therefore not within his free decision. They belong to the area of fate. Second, it was his free decision how to act in the given situation —he could give in to his excitement (touch the women, expose himself to them), or ignore it. The young man decided not to give in, especially since he had emotional ties elsewhere. Because this was his conviction, and because he acted according to his conviction within his area of freedom, there was no reason for guilt feelings. He reported later that the arousal symptoms diminished.

Dreams, too, belong to the area of fate; we have no freedom to choose our dreams. What is within our power however, is the importance we attach to them, our interpretations. This allows the therapist to shift the patients' attention from the area of fate to that of freedom, and thus help find positive and meaningful attitudes toward choices made.

Case No. 2

After a furious marital battle, the wife dreams of a deep abyss that has opened between herself and her husband. She asks if this means her marriage can no longer be saved. But another interpretation is possible. Could the dream not have told her that she ought to look for a way to circumvent the gulf or, together with her husband, build a bridge?

This is not a mere reinterpretation of a situation by the logotherapist, but a motivation for patients or suffering persons to discover its positive aspects. Underlying is the assumption that we are free to shape our lives, at least to some extent, and not become fatalistic.

If the wife has the attitude that "nothing can be done" because she and her husband are separated by an unbridgeable abyss then, and only then, can the marriage no longer be saved. As long as she sees the challenge of the situation and mobilizes all her strength to find a solution, she has a chance to bridge the gap.

Fatalism is a dangerous consequence of determinism. If practically all our thinking and acting are determined by past and present influences most psychotherapeutic efforts (which aim at changing ourselves for the better) would be useless.

Logotherapy opposes an absolute determinism that is bound to end in fatalism, as well as the principle of homeostasis, widely accepted by psychology. This principle, in various forms, holds that we have all sorts of needs that push us toward gratification of those needs. Unless they are gratified, our inner equilibrium is thrown off and we become sick or abnormal.

The homeostasis principle is true for animals and also for infants whose dimension of the spirit exists only as potential. The baby cries when hungry, sleeps contentedly when full. The more the human spirit develops, the more the homeostasis principle loses validity; the goal is no longer simple gratification of needs, short-range pleasure, abreaction of drives, and the whole range of motivational theories. The dimension of a free spirit helps us detach from the determinism and automatism of the homeostasis principle which stands opposed to freedom. If there is freedom in choosing attitudes, we can also choose whether we want gratification. We can say "no" to gratification without being considered sick or abnormal. Motivation then follows another and higher criterion than pressure to gratification, and this Frankl calls the "will to meaning."

There are numerous "proofs" proofs of the existence of the will to meaning. I mention only one. A retired physician decided to go to a nearby home for the blind to comfort the residents. To his surprise he discovered that they did not suffer as much from blindness as from meaninglessness. They had no tasks, no goals, felt useless and unfulfilled, empty, and frustrated. The residents were not interested when the physician talked about their blindness: they listened eagerly when he suggested what they could do, even small tasks like arranging activities for an afternoon.

What the doctor discovered is the fact that we have a dimension that helps us transcend ourselves and our needs, toward goals beyond ourselves, toward meanings higher than personal needs. What the doctor saw was that nothing, not even blindness, is as difficult to bear as meaninglessness of living, the "existential frustration," as Frankl calls it.

Existential frustration or, to use another logotherapeutic term, "existential vacuum," has increased rapidly during the past decades, and the problem of apparent meaninglessness of life has affected the populations of our day. The sufferers are by no means always poor, old, sick, or lonely. They often live in affluence and suffer from doubts and feelings of meaninglessness. They are taken care of without doing much in return, their needs are met, they have social security.

Nothing is wrong with affluence and social security but there is ample evidence that they may result in mass neurosis and an alarming increase in psychopathological illness as evidenced in drug abuse, suicides, and criminality. Homeostasis is not sufficient for a healthy and happy life, or we would have more healthy people than sick ones. The opposite is true: the more we try to create an inner balance through outer influence, the more we make people into "reacting" or "abreacting" automatons

Figure 1. Consequences of Assumption about Human Nature

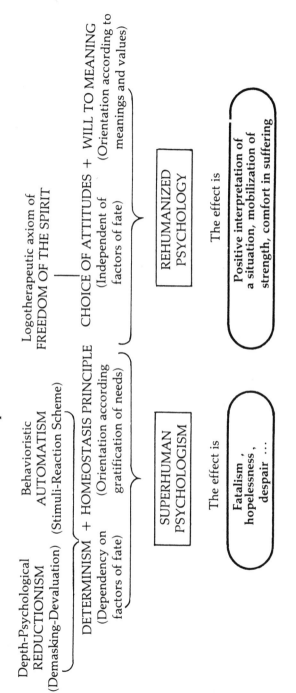

into need-gratification machines, into "nothing but" consumers. The human image becomes subhuman, the truly human dimension eliminated. Determinism (stressed by psychologists), fatalism (accepted by patients), and subhumanism (promoted by an affluent society) is a triple tragedy whose victims no psychotherapists can cure unless today's crisis prompts them to rethink the concepts of human nature.

How can the physician or psychologist counter existential frustration—the "suffering of a meaningless life"? This suffering spreads especially among the young, and fosters a variety of psychological illnesses. Meaning cannot be prescribed: what is meaningful for one is not for another. A glimpse at possible choices, pointing to a range of free decisions as indicated in logotherapeutic counseling, opens up approaches. Possible choices must be directed to a *personal* goal and various paths toward this goal indicated. Possible choices without a definite goal usually have little therapeutic use.

That is why it is not enough to make patients aware that they are free to act and find new attitudes when facing an unchangeable situation. Their choices have to be linked to a meaning, a goal, a task.

Case No. 3

I once counseled an alcoholic after her detoxification. The woman was all right but then she was fired from her job, suddenly and without explanation. She probably was considered unstable, and it seemed preferable to let her go while she was healthy, rather than during a relapse when she could claim sick leave. For the woman this was a blow of fate, and she was in danger of giving up, to see all her efforts as pointless, and in despair start drinking again. I kept almost daily contact with her to prevent a relapse.

It was not difficult to separate fate from the free area: having been fired was fate, irreversible; her free choice was to start drinking again, or to stay sober, to give up or to look for another job. The difficulty began when she asked, in a fatalistic mood, why remain sober and look for work? She obviously remained an alcoholic, regarded so by others, as the firing had shown. The question of meaning had to be raised; was there a goal worth pursuing, a value that made the effort worthwhile?

It was a great struggle, but together we wrenched meaning from her situation, a goal worth fighting for, namely to prove her employer was wrong.

It took half a year for her to find new work, because no one liked to employ a former alcoholic. Even after she started working she needed the most intensive support to stick it out. Some mornings she called me to say she had no strength to get out of bed and to go to work. "All right," I told her then, "you can spend a nice morning in bed and admit to your former employer that he was right and you no longer are capable of working, or you can bring yourself to get up, by your own free choice, and prove that your dismissal was based on a false prognosis." Thus I kept challenging her, and she chose the positive course. Today she no longer needs this proof of her ability to work, she enjoys her job, has formed firm ground under her feet, and the danger of a relapse has greatly diminished. It is not always easy to see meaning in a situation. In hopeless pain and suffering there seems hardly any goal worth pursuing, but even so the choice of attitude remains open. Frankl speaks here of "realizing our attitudinal values."

What he means is our attitude toward unchangeable facts that make us unhappy. A family breaks up, a sickness is incurable, a professional career has ended, a natural catastrophe has destroyed a home, or financial necessity forces a bitter austerity. Self-inflicted guilt, too, may have irrevocable consequences which keep reminding us of the terrible event. Many people, under such circumstances, do not want to keep on living because all is lost. This unhealthy attitude increases unhappiness and makes everything worse.

Logotherapy helps by making people aware that they have one choice left, regardless how irrevocable the facts: their choice of attitude toward such situations. They can accept them or condemn themselves or the world; they can show courage and trust in the future, or despair. This is *their* decision: the cruelest fate does not have the power to decide how they will face it. One thing, however, is certain: if we find a positive attitude in the face of extremely negative circumstances, we find strong comfort in that we need not lose our self-respect: we can even proudly bear our suffering, with dignity, and be an example to others in their tragedies.

The term "attitudinal values" implies the high value attached to positive human attitudes taken in apparently hopeless situations. Often they are the only way out—giving fate a positive direction through inner strength. Only a positive attitude toward suffering will produce a positive turn while blind despair sinks ever deeper into distress and guilt.

A turn to the positive is a turn to the meaningful, a readiness to make the best of an unchangeable situation, to extract and fulfill a meaning within it. Some people have discovered incredible meanings in abysmal situations like Helen Keller, deaf and blind since her second year, an inspiration for millions. Many have borne witness that human beings are able to turn suffering into achievement by discovering meaning behind suffering, and thus reassurance. They show that the suffering person, more than anyone else, can offer hope and comfort to others.

Case No. 4

My patient was a man whose much younger wife had left him and an infant and was unwilling to return. She let him know that he was too old for her and she wanted a divorce. The man was devastated, developed a heart condition, and looked as if he would not live long. It seemed impossible to find a goal that would give his life new meaning. Wife and child had been the entire content of his life, his sorrow sapped his strength. He could not think of anything else. It was necessary, therefore, to link suffering itself with some meaning he could accept. His choices were limited because he could not do anything to win his wife back. I offered him another, imaginary choice: "When two people promise each other to stay together under all circumstances, and one of them breaks the promise and leaves, then the one who leaves presumably feels pleasure, and the other must suffer. But the one who left is guilty of a broken promise, while the other has a clear conscience. If you had the choice, what would you have chosen: suffering and a clear conscience, or pleasure and guilt?"

He decided in favor of his own role, the role of the one left behind. He said that if one of the partners had to suffer, he was prepared to be the one, that his suffering did not seem completely meaningless if it was the price for keeping his promise. This was the beginning: accepting fate and bearing his loneliness with courage.

The need to be comforted is not restricted to situations of unavoidable suffering. Those who can change and improve things occasionally need comfort, too, to face fate in a positive way. Frankl speaks in such cases of mobilizing the "defiant power of the human spirit," which—more than physical and psychic strength—can overcome obstacles and conquer difficulties.

The greatest obstacles are our own weaknesses, the greatest difficulty is conquering our faults. If the freedom of the human spirit is a true axiom, there is no limit to finding new attitudes to external suffering as well as to inner weaknesses. We have free choice about our flaws, too: we can submit to them or defy them. We are not helpless victims.

All specifically logotherapeutic methods aim at freeing patients from their determining factors and filling the newly freed area with potential or real meanings. They are more than psychotherapeutic methods—they are motivations to shaping lives, an education to meaningful living. Logotherapeutic counseling does not deal primarily with what is sick in patients; it teaches them to use what is healthy. Counseling is focused not on the latent abnormal and perverse, but on positive and worthwhile potentials which can be developed.

Because logotherapists work within the area of freedom of the spirit, they communicate this to patients. "You have a problem, a symptom, but no one forces you to fear it, to consider it important, to keep watching it, submit to it, or end your life because of it. You may just as well accept it, transform it into something positive, ignore it, even laugh at it!"

Laughing at symptoms is used in the logotherapeutic technique of paradoxical intention.* It is a classical example of the mobilization of our "defiant power" to overcome weaknesses, and thus turn negative events that are avoidable toward the positive.

---

*A thorough discussion of paradoxical intention, dereflection, and modification of attitudes, is found in *Meaningful Living* by Elisabeth Lukas, an Institute of Logotherapy Press book, published by Grove Press, New York.

Patients who suffer from unnecessary or exaggerated fears and compulsions learn to make fun of their fears by wishing (paradoxically) for exactly what they fear. Humor and exaggeration are essential in this technique. Patients who are afraid to cross bridges, are encouraged to do this with the firm intent and

Figure 2. Logotherapeutic Approach to Suffering

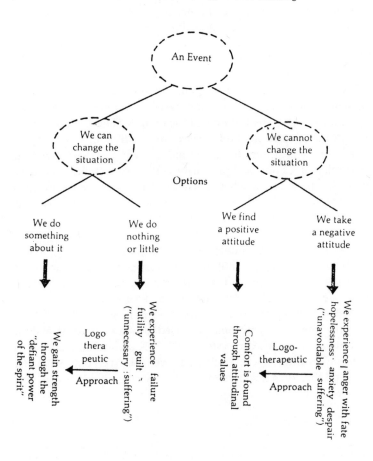

wish to fall into the water often and with great aplomb. Those who feel compelled to constantly check if the gas is turned off and the door locked, are invited to leave the house with the firm wish that the time finally has arrived for the building to burn down or be burglarized. Students who tremble at the thought of stuttering at their orals are told to go to the exam with the firm intent to prove to their professor that they are the greatest stutterers of all time. The ridiculousness of the paradoxical wish is part of the method—ridicule is not directed at the patients but at their symptoms. They can conquer fear as they laugh—they cannot fear what they find amusing.

Fear is part of fate, regardless how it originates. Patients cannot choose to have or not have fears. What they are free to choose is response to fear, either run from it or face it. I have often accompanied patients in buses and subways, in crowded department stores, in elevators, to practice paradoxical intention with them. It always turned out that the fastest and most enduring success is achieved by those who (in the dimension of the spirit) can distance themselves from their fears (in the dimension of their psyche), and also possess enough humor to think up humorous paradoxical formulations. Humor is a form of "defiant power" and can mitigate suffering caused by our own weaknesses.

Case No. 5

A young mother sometimes calls her little son "my little soccer ball" which goes back to our paradoxical formulations. The mother wanted a child for years. When the baby came he was premature and had to remain in an incubator for six weeks. When he finally was handed to the mother she developed a deadly fear of handling him. Every nursing and diaper change was a catastrophe. She always was beset by dread that this baby could slip through her hands and be hurt.

The father asked me for help. I visited the woman regularly and practiced handling the child while saying such paradoxical sentences as, "Now come, little one, I'll play soccer with you, I finally have a toy all for myself, I always wanted this—perhaps I can score a goal with you today!" The mother laughed and cried at the same time, but as long as the baby was "her soccer ball," she could pick him up, turn him over, and eventually even bathe him (the bathtub was the "goal"). Later I only needed to call her and ask how the "soccer ball" was doing, and she laughed and said she was improving daily.

The boy has become a robust little fellow, and the worry of the mother has diminished to normal levels. Whatever triggered her fear—her character structure, a latent psychosis during pregnancy, separation from the baby after birth—no longer matters. The symptom disappeared, no others turned up, and the family has been spared a long and complicated therapy.

While paradoxical intention ridicules the symptoms, another logotherapeutic method, *dereflection*, seemingly ignores them.

A number of difficulties in normal life—psychosomatic illnesses, paranoia, or fixation on a thought—exist as long as we pay attention to them, become worse if we brood about them (in "hyperreflection"), but disappear when ignored. The problem is that most people cannot ignore them. In these cases the logotherapeutic technique of dereflection is a great help, and it is amazing how many severe difficulties can be eliminated. The goal is to find a thought content that is so impelling and meaningful that, in the decisive moment, patients will focus attention on it, and thus dereflect from self-observation and the fearful expectation of symptoms—which do not occur.

Dereflection has become known in the treatment of sleep disturbances and sexual dysfunction. In both cases patients try to force a physical reaction, and the result is exactly the opposite. Patients are then directed to think about something else. The natural, healthy reaction (falling asleep, erection, orgasm) occurs when not intended. That is why patients are told to think through a certain problem before falling asleep, or are forbidden to have intercourse while paying attention to their partner, leading to the desired result.

Here is a relatively simple problem demonstrating the broad application of dereflection.

Case No. 6

A little girl had the greatest difficulty in learning how to swim. The mother who had learned dereflection in conquering her own sleep disturbances, tried the same idea on her daughter.

The girl did not learn swimming because she anxiously observed the rhythms of her motions which prevented natural body movements and landed her under the water. This increased her anxiety and exaggerated her self-observation which in turn interfered with arm and leg rhythms.

The mother took a tape recorder to the beach and played a cassette fairy tale loud enough so the girl could hear it while learning to swim. She learned it in four days and on the fifth had to be admonished not to venture too far out.

Interested listening automatically achieved a reduction of "hyperreflection" (exaggerated attention) and hyperintention (exaggerated wish to enforce something). While the child thought of the fairy tale, and not of her swimming, natural body movement took over.

This simple example confutes the homeostasis principle. Today we are primarily concerned with self-finding, self-strengthening, self-actualization, and similar ego-centered goals, and yet, an exaggerated occupation with the "beloved ego" is harmful. We are basically self-transcending beings, focussing on a reality—even by way of a fairy tale.

Suffering or neurotic persons, too, may become healthy to the degree they direct their attention to the reality beyond themselves and ignore the ego with all its weaknesses and problems. In therapy, it is dangerous to encourage unhealthy focus on the ego or to arouse self-pity in suffering people. In disregarding the patients' self-transcending qualities, we feed an egoism that can be fatal to spiritual life.

Therapeutic counseling places a heavy responsibility on therapists. They must provide comfort—and refrain from taking away comfort. I am talking about the "iatrogenic damage" (doctor-caused damage) that did not exist before consultation. The damage can be the result of something the therapist says or does (or does not say or do) which the patient misunderstands: people can become sick if the visit to the doctor leads them to suspect that they *are* sick.

Such suggestive or placebo effects are well-known in medical circles. In psychotherapy the suggestibility of psychologically unstable or suffering persons may be much higher, so feedback effect of therapist on patient is greater than in ordinary medical practice. "Self-fulfilling prophecies" can have positive or negative effects. Positively, they contain the chance to improve wellbeing; negatively, the words of the therapist, however meant, may create hopelessness.

I once heard a lecture of a well-known psychotherapist on the subject, "Are depressions curable?" One must assume that many people in the audience came because they suffered from depression or had family members afflicted with this problem. The speaker, however, paid no attention to this consideration, and explained for more than two hours, along strict deterministic lines, how depression can be predicted from early childhood deficits, how they recur throughout the lives of such "victims of childhood experiences," and have all the more terrifying consequences the more the patient tries to repress them. Eventually, the speaker said, such and such a percentage of patients was bound to end in suicide because they were not able to suffer through depressions.

During the entire lecture I desperately tried to understand how a therapist could give such depressing and hopeless scientific explanations before an audience that might not be able to assimilate such material. The reaction was predictable— distressed silence, an occasional sobbing, moist eyes.

Case No. 7

I invited one woman who seemed especially confused to our counseling center and tried in a logotherapeutic talk to repair the consequences of the lecture.

The woman had twice gone through a professional crisis. First, she had to give up a choice job as stewardess because of age; subsequently, as a telephone operator, she was badly treated and had to look for other work. Both times she wept for days but developed new strength and found a new job. A friend had teased her, suggesting she might become depressed. She went to the lecture to learn more about depression. So far, there was no trace of abnormal behavior, no indication of an endogenous depression, at most a slight and passing reactive depression in connection with job disappointments but not requiring professional help. After the lecture a dangerous hyperreflection had set in, brooding about an apparently depressive tendency which could lead to a negative self-fulfilling prophecy. Nothing could more readily lead to a deep depression than constant self-observation for symptoms of depression. Anticipatory anxiety had started its neurotic cycle and could have catastrophic consequences. The woman was not depressed, she was iatrogenically damaged by someone whose task it was to help people in search of comfort.

To correct iatrogenic damage a technique was applied which in logotherapy is called "modulation of attitudes." What frightened the woman was the following consideration: "I've had two depressions, so a third will come!" Her fatalism was reinforced by what she heard about recurring depressions.

It was necessary to explain to her the difference between endogenous (biologically caused) and reactive depressions (a response to an event), and to confirm what she knew before the lecture: that her depressive phases had not come out of a clear sky, but were linked with a problem she faced and were therefore quite natural. This reassured her but she anxiously inquired whether her depressions would recur.

Now was the time to modulate her attitudes from the negative to the positive. I did not say: "Well, you had depressions twice before, this of course is something to think about." Instead I said: "Twice you have overcome depressive phases without help from anyone, that's a remarkable achievement, and shows how much will and courage to live are in you! Without these crises you would not even know your strength, but your suffering has shown you how secure you are. You can face the future with confidence! Anyone who finds a new beginning after a deep setback need not fear anything." This broke the iatrogenic damage. The woman overcame the dangerous conclusion, "I had two depressions and a third one will come," and told herself, "I have come out of two depressions and I'll come out of a third, if need be!" This was the turning-point to her problem. If there was to be a self-fulfilling prophecy, it was in a positive direction. After a few more logotherapeutic talks, I discharged her, she was well and stable and did not think of possible future depressions. I never had to search into her past, analyze her childhood, examine ungratified needs, or teach new behavior. None of the widely used psychotechniques were required, only a bit of logotherapy and human empathy.

Paramahansa Yogananda, in his book, "Scientific Meditation for Health," writes:

"A room, darkened for centuries, can immediately be made bright when one lets light enter but not when one attempts to drive out the darkness."

These words are a suitable parable of the logotherapeutic appeal to modern psychology which too often tries, in long-lasting procedures, to drive out "the darkness of the human heart," and forgets to let enter "the light in the human spirit." A small word of comfort into the large coffer of psychotherapeutic methods can be like a ray of light suddenly revealing what was hidden: that there is meaning in your suffering when you make the effort to find it.

CHAPTER TWO

THE BEST POSSIBLE HELP

Psychotherapeutic counseling consists of three phases: diagnosis, therapy, and follow-up.

In the diagnostic phase the therapist tries to get information in the medical history through examinations, questionnaires, tests, and in-depth interviews.

The therapeutic phase is to help clients to overcome their difficulties through psychological techniques, direct and indirect counseling, medication, dialogues, and cooperative efforts.

In the follow-up phase the therapist wants to keep the clients psychologically healthy and independent after conclusion of therapy. This may include follow-up dialogues and referrals.

These phases have undergone changes. Fifty years ago, the diagnostic phase was exceedingly long, the therapeutic phase short, and follow-up practically nonexistent. Today, the therapeutic phase has overtaken the diagnostic in significance while the importance of the follow-up is only beginning to be understood.

The success of each phase depends on the favorable termination of the previous one. Therapy will fail after incorrect diagnosis, no follow-up is possible after an unsuccessful therapy. Each phase has its own methods which differ according to the school of therapy used, but in recent years methods have generally improved. Each phase also has its dangers which may disturb, and even break the contact between therapist and client. The situation improves as the human relationship between the two becomes firmer. The danger of a breakup is greatest during the diagnostic phase, but resistance may occur during therapy, and saturation during the follow-up. Because therapists are dependent on client response, they too may feel uneasy and even hostile if there is no response—evasive answers during the diagnostic phase, opposition to help offered during therapy, and lack of feedback during follow-up.

In applying logotherapeutic principles during the three phases, one must realize that there is no such thing as a specifically logotherapeutic diagnosis; in therapy more is needed than logotherapeutic techniques; and the follow-up requires knowledge that goes beyond logotherapy. While it is true that pure logotherapy is not enough for psychological counseling, it is also true that such counseling is incomplete without application of logotherapeutic principles. These principles are not universal guidelines but a professional supplement to optimal living, regardless of the approach used.

This chapter discusses the "best possible help" in logo-therapeutic counseling. In the diagnostic phase it would be not to cause "iatrogenic" problems, and to counteract "hyperreflection." In the therapeutic phase clients are helped through specific logotherapeutic techniques and modulation of attitudes. During the follow-up, attention is focused on helping clients find specific meanings and broaden their values.

THE DIAGNOSTIC PHASE

During the diagnostic phase the counselor attempts to identify the client's problems and reasons why they were not overcome. Counselors look for symptoms and weaknesses, for past disturbances and traumas, for current hardships and troubles. Many counselors assume that a problem can be mastered only after origins are understood, and a destructive development corrected only after causes are uncovered.

While this assumption is correct in theory, practicing counselors realize that the diagnostic phase is often confusing to clients. The probing during this phase does help counselors get a clearer picture of the problem and a better idea about a functional therapy plan. The more they learn, the better they can fit the client in a program that takes into account cause and effect, sickness and treatment, and thus facilitate further work. Once such a program is established, many counselors tend to stick with it even when subsequent information does not fit. They are inclined not to "hear" information that is in variance with their program, and pay special attention to information that is in accord with it.

Figure 3. Course of Counseling

Diagnostic Phase	Therapy Phase	Follow-up Phase
The therapist gets as much information as possible about the client.	The therapist gives the client as much help as possible.	The therapist wants to discharge the client as independent and well as 'possible.
Means: Questions and answers.	Means: Offers and acceptance of therapy.	Means: Checking and feedback.
Methods: History of difficulties, examination, questionnaires, consideration of outer circumstances, listing symptoms.	Methods: Therapeutic techniques, counseling, therapy plans, including meditation exercises, concrete information, discussion.	Methods: Occasional contacts in person or by telephone.

This observation is not meant as criticism. Human problems are often so complex that counselors have to simplify or lose sight of the whole picture. I merely wish to draw attention to the consequences of the diagnostic phase for clients. Their problems have occupied their minds for a long time, perhaps for years before professional help. Because they were not able to solve their problems, these seem unsolvable, and they look to counselors full of hope, doubt, and anxiety. In this situation every word and question of the counselor is highly portentous, anything said or done provokes anxiety, especially if it is not clearly understood by the client. Some clients wait breathlessly for the counselor's decision to see if they can be helped at all, and in what way, or whether they may have a "defect" or are "abnormal."

Because counselors, during the diagnostic phase, concentrate on getting a clear picture of the case, they may not pay much attention to the effects their questions and statements have on the clients. At the same time, the clients listen over-anxiously to the counselors who seem to pronounce a verdict. During this period of cautious first contacts, clients may suffer irreparable damage unnoticed by counselors. Iatrogenic neuroses and hyperreflection can be avoided by the sensitivity of the therapist during quiet listening and words should be used with foresight. As mentioned in the last chapter, iatrogenic neurosis is a neurosis caused by the physician, psychologist, or counselor. It may be triggered by what the physician does or says which the patients, justifiably or not, interpret as "bad news," and thus the problem in intensified. A neurologist told a woman suffering from a slight confusion that she had an "attack of paranoia." Her initial symptoms were completely cleared up by medication but the fear of a renewed attack of paranoia darkened her life years after the episode. A long period of anxiety, insecurity, and self-doubt undermined her self-confidence and prevented her from enjoying life. Although she never had a relapse, and it is not even certain that she actually had a genuine attack of paranoia, she now suffers from iatrogenic neurosis caused by a few words of the neurologist who treated her correctly, freeing her medically from symptoms that had brought her to him.

An iatrogenic neurosis starts with the concurrence of two factors: a careless remark or behavior by the physician, and hyperreflection by the patient. Had the neurologist been more careful with his remarks or had the patient not placed so much weight on them, the subsequent neurosis would have been avoided.

People who lack self-confidence and are psychologically unstable tend to hyperreflect: they pay exaggerated attention to details. This "circling around oneself" is one of the most dangerous and unhealthy attitudes, the "enemy number one" of health. Hyperreflection turns minute everyday problems into catastrophes, and minor obstacles become insurmountable hurdles. The life of a person caught in hyperreflection becomes a confusion of countless terrible possibilities which *could* happen, and are a burden before they ever *do* happen.

Persons constantly worrying about their wellbeing will never feel well, and those continuously watching themselves for symptoms of sickness are already sick.

Psychologically healthy persons are not without problems but limit their concerns to those over which they have some control: they look for transcending goals when faced with an inalterable difficult situation.

Counselors looking for useful information during the diagnostic phase must watch themselves (to avoid iatrogenic neuroses) and watch the clients (to counteract hyperreflection).

IATROGENIC NEUROSES

Iatrogenic problems cannot be avoided by *not* making diagnostic statements because the counselor's silence can also cause anxiety. Nor are they avoided by minimizing what clients find burdensome and significant. They may feel that the counselor does not take them seriously or does not understand them.

The counselor is well advised to stick cautiously to the truth but present it within the framework of what is meaningful in this case, stressing positive aspects.

I often have to tell parents that their child is not suited for the academic high school, the pathway to a college education in Germany. To tell parents the "truth" that their child's intelligence quotient is too low for admittance to a preparatory school for college could cause an iatrogenic problem. They may consider their child "stupid" or "unfit," and thus block the child's potential development. I am not violating the truth by advising the parents to forego an academic education for the child whose talent lies along a practical trade where it is likely to be successful.Parents need the confidence that their child will find its way in life, and this reassurance means more than verdicts based on questionable psychological tests.

A "truthful" answer may also be damaging to clients who ask what's "wrong" with them. It is no lie to answer this question within a relative framework that includes not only what's wrong but also what's right with the client.

I once told an extremely frustrated and shy young woman that she was a pleasant exception to the prevalence of excessively self-centered people around, and that I wanted to help strengthen her assertiveness only to protect her in this egotistic world, and not to change her personality. This "diagnosis" alone lifted her self-confidence and laid the foundation for further logotherapy. To diagnose her as suffering from a serious inferiority complex would not have helped. It might have helped *me* develop a therapy plan against a problem that I had intensified.

Iatrogenic problems can be avoided if the diagnosis is linked to thoughts that prompt a smile in the client. Those who can smile about their problems are on their way toward overcoming them.

An elderly man asked me anxiously if his pattern of depressive phases would recur for the rest of his life. According to test results I held in my hand this was likely. I told him: "No one can tell with certainty whether a depression will come back. But we do know for certain that you have come out of your 'downs' every time and lived in long periods of 'ups.' You have so many healthy ups ahead of you that you had better start thinking soon about what you are going to do with all this healthy time." The patient acknowledged my answer with a quiet smile although he well understood the truth.

Truth is never clear-cut, not in religion, not in physics, and not in psychology. Who can tell which one of the two drunks speaks the truth when one says, "Isn't it terrible, we have hardly sat down on this bench and our bottle is half empty," and the other, "I don't know what you're complaining about. We've sat here for quite a while and our bottle is still half full."

In the human dimension, truth is always more than truth. It moves toward happiness or suffering, satisfaction or despair. The success of therapy may depend on how the counselor handles "truth" in the diagnostic phase—presenting it in a form that enables the client to accept it with confidence.

HYPERREFLECTION

Clients tend to suffer from hyperreflection to some degree before they enter the consulting room, whether they are really sick or just imagine they are, and whether their sickness is serious or not. They have lived with their problem, it has occupied their thoughts. In this regard, their difficulty is not determined by how real it is but how anxiously they reflect upon it.

Counselors begin the diagnostic phase by inquiring about the clients' problems in all possible connections. They ask a woman suffering from insomnia in what circumstances she has trouble falling asleep, what brings on sleeplessness, how long it has been a problem, in what nightly rhythms it occurs, what medication has been tried, and whatever else seems pertinent. Or the counselor may ask a man with marriage problems how he met his wife, about her good or bad qualities, and how the marriage has developed, his expectations, and how far he is prepared to meet her wishes.

Such questions intensify the client's initial tendency to hyperreflection. The sleepless woman will observe her sleeping patterns more closely and from all possible angles, and the unhappily married man will keep analyzing himself and his wife, reflecting more and more upon the troubled relationship.

To make things worse, in inquiring about the development of the trouble, counselors—looking for possible causes—are likely to pay attention to all that has been abnormal and ailing. Thus clients get the impression that so much is wrong that they have no other choice but to be sick, making them sicker and more discouraged.

The result is that the diagnostic phase helps the counselor get much-needed information, but at the expense of intensifying the problem. The therapeutic phase will reduce the heightened hyperreflection and this is one of the direct or indirect goals of all therapies. Even psychoanalysis, which tends to encourage hyperreflection by persistently probing the causes of the present symptoms, in a successful therapy reaches a saturation point when clients turn away from reconstructing the past, and thus reduce hyperreflection. But no therapy can speedily eliminate tendencies to hyperreflect. Even after symptoms have been eliminated, clients tend to place undue importance on trivialities, and this may become a hazard in the follow-up. My experiences and those of my colleagues have shown that incidents of relapse are incomparably higher in cases where the counselor started the follow-up with a client still absorbed in a high level of hyperreflection.

Figure 4. The Danger of Relapse Exists After a
Steep Increase of Hyperreflection During the Diagnostic Phase

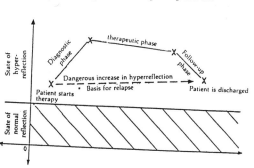

Clients who are hardly interested in follow-up because they are occupied with new tasks, rarely think of previous problems, and don't want to be reminded of them, can be discharged as safe and stable. On the other hand, clients during the follow-up who still think about former problems as under temporary control but likely to reemerge are in transition and could relapse at the slightest provocation.

I tried to find ways to rapidly reduce the clients' hyperreflection before discharge. Today I know that it is wrong to allow hyperreflection to build up in the diagnostic phase and then think about methods of reducing it during and after therapy. The basic concepts of logotherapy have helped me to see that hyperreflection must be counteracted right from the start, even at the expense of information which can be procured later. This procedure presents a dilemma for counselors because they need to get early diagnostic information and must ask certain questions and conduct certain inquiries, but this can be solved by a technique which I call "alternate diagnosis."

Figure 5. Healthy Lowering of Hyperreflection (After Alternate Diagnosis) Provides a Stable Base During the Follow-up

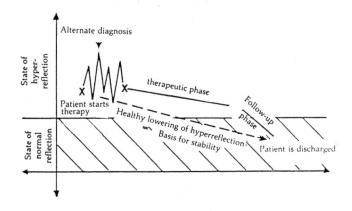

The alternate diagnosis technique satisfies both requirements of the diagnostic phase: it allows gathering information without raising the client's level of hyperreflection. In this technique the counselor's interest alternates between gathering information and dereflecting the client from problems toward positive life contents.

In the case of the woman suffering from insomnia, alternate diagnosis may take the following form:

A. Query about frequency of sleep disturbances. Talks about such subjects as day and night rhythms.

B. Query about activities which the client likes to do and to which she could turn in sleepless hours (reading, listening to music, solving puzzles, cooking).

C. Discussion of these activities and her experiences with them.

D. Query about connections between emotionally strenuous human encounters and the occurrence of sleep disturbances.

E. General dialogue about the client's encounters with relatives, friends, acquaintances.

F. Discussion about possible links between some of these persons and the client's hobbies, inclinations, and interests.

In this example, two questions (A and D) dealt with the client's symptoms, the other four were set up to counteract excessive attention to sleep problems, and to focus interest on other, more healthy areas of life. Every question about sleeplessness might have increased hyperreflection, but other questions helped lower it again so that the client entered her second therapeutic phase at a level of hyperreflection no higher than she had brought to the diagnostic phase in the first place (see Figure 5).

It sometimes happens that during an alternate diagnosis the hyperreflection dissolves, and the clients see their difficulties with new eyes, now entirely manageable. Though rare, it indicates that this form of initial contact contains therapeutic elements not evident in regular diagnostic inquiry.

Case No. 8

A young music teacher worried about occasional "blocks." He was a busy man but sometimes felt "burned out." He would sit listless, staring in the air.

Neurological and psychological tests found nothing. He had read in the literature, and found that sudden mood changes could be the first indications of schizophrenia.

I was tempted to inquire more about his mysterious blocks but was hesitant to intensify his attention on them. I got the necessary information from colleagues and the tests they had given him, and asked him about the positive aspects of his life. Few questions were necessary. The young man proudly reported his activities. He liked to work with his students, organized student orchestras which he conducted, and took several classes to further his education. Weekends he visited his hometown and a girl whom his parents considered their future daughter-in-law. He loved to dance and went out almost every night. He was also an enthusiastic tennis player and skier. He saved for a motorboat on which he planned to take summer trips along the coast. He was widely read and asked my opinion on various favorite authors.

For almost two hours he reported about his activities. Then he became quiet and seemed to remember why he had come. "Your vitality is amazing," I told him, "I can't understand how you can keep going without a rest." He thought a while, and then said, "Well, yes, the blocks I told you about...that's sort of a pause...maybe these are periods of rest my body requires..." I admitted that this may be so—he was not a machine that could run day and night. He thought a while longer, and said, "I really do a lot, don't I, why do I worry about these few moments when I come to a stop?"

He seemed embarrassed. "I now feel almost silly to have worried about it. Well, anyway, thanks for listening. It was unnecessary to tell you about what I'm doing, but I see now that I have no reason to be dissatisfied." "Well, then maybe it was not all that unnecessary," I said, and asked him to come again when he was worried. But he never returned.

I reported the outcome to my colleagues. The first suspected unconscious guilt that drove the young man to a "flight from something" and wanted to uncover the causes of guilt. The other one had intended to send the client to a clinic to check if his blocks had an organic origin in the brain.

I suspected that the young man's explanations during my "positive diagnostic" were not far off the mark. In any case, further therapy seemed unnecessary.

Some of my colleagues object to alternate diagnosis because it "prolongs the diagnostic phase unnecessarily." It is true that alternate diagnosis slows down the collecting of information but this is not an "unnecessary" delay. It facilitates the transition to the therapeutic phase, and the information which during the diagnostic phase seems "superfluous" becomes highly useful in the follow-up when clients are led toward meaningful goals and a wide variety of values.

It is important that the counseling dialogue right from the start of the diagnostic phase include the healthy and positive aspects of the clients' life. This procedure protects them from additional iatrogenic disturbances, and also counteracts hyper-reflection by showing them—after their problems are cleared up—how much life still has to offer.

THE THERAPEUTIC PHASE

During the therapeutic phase logotherapists have at their disposal two specific logotherapeutic techniques (paradoxical intention and dereflection) and the unspecific logotherapeutic procedure of modulation of attitudes. These three techniques have been extensively described in my book, *Meaningful Living*. Referring to problems of human suffering one may say: Paradoxical intention helps in cases where the suffering is caused by feeling trapped in a vicious cycle, such as fears of obsessions; dereflection aims at reducing unnecessary suffering; and modulation of attitudes is a tool against inevitable suffering.

PARADOXICAL INTENTION

Paradoxical intention is based on Frankl's early discovery that for phobias and obsessions the best possible advice is not to run away from the fear or fight the compulsions but, instead, to "intend" or wish to happen what is feared. A wish and a fear are mutually exclusive: What we wish to happen cannot be feared. The burden is lifted and the psychological consequences disappear. A phobic woman who walks into an elevator with the firm intention to collapse on every floor, is not able to do it because she is no longer overwhelmed by the extreme fear which could alone cause a psychosomatic collapse. That she feels "funny" to be wishing for something which for years she feared, does not matter. On the contrary: the less seriously she takes her attempt, the more she can "smile" about it; the more distance she places between her self and her symptoms, the more she frees herself for becoming well.

How paradoxical intention is used in therapy is well documented in logotherapy literature. In counseling, and even among lay people, application is not limited to "sickness." A wife kept threatening her husband with divorce and several times began to pack her suitcases until he gave in to her wishes. One day, instead of participating in the "crisis," he cheerfully helped her pack, suggesting many heavy things to take along, and offering her three extra suitcases, until they both dissolved in laughter. A father whose boys constantly fought each other, suggested just at the crucial moment he would take over the burden of their battle and beat them up himself. When they stared at him in surprise, he suggested calling in a neighbor, a boxing champion, who "could do the job professionally and would not charge a cent for it."

A variation of paradoxical intention can be used in many cases where undesirable behavior patterns have developed.

Case No. 9

The parents were in despair over the continual lies of their little son. He always blamed other children for his mishaps. He spilled ink on his notebook and accused a schoolmate. He tore his pants and told his parents he had been attacked on the street. The parents worried about character development.

I, too, was concerned. Since he apparently was not mature enough to take responsibility for his actions, I felt it was better for him not to explain anything rather than accuse others. I advised the parents paradoxically not to ask the boy how the damage was done, but to pretend the causes were irrelevant. Rather they should discuss with him how to repair the damage—rewrite the soiled pages in his notebook, help as much as he could to mend, wash and iron his pants. I suspected that if he was not pressed for an explanation, he would sooner or later feel the need to confide in the parents.

The first opportunity presented itself the next evening. The boy had broken the glass of his wristwatch. He had thrown the glass into the garbage can and hid the watch behind his back. The mother pretended not to notice. Later she went to his room and found him at his desk holding the watch, swallowing his tears. "Oh," she said nonchalantly, "the watch has no glass. If we had the fragments we could try to glue them together." She left the room, and after a while the boy came out of his room, not saying anything and fished the glass splinters from the garbage can. "Fine," the mother said, "now get some glue and scotch tape and fix the watch." The boy flabbergasted that he wasn't scolded busied himself to fix the glass as well as he could. The incident was not mentioned.

When the mother, as she did every night, went to his bed to kiss him goodnight, the boy pulled her down and whispered what had happened. He had put the watch at the edge of the playground and stepped on it by mistake. Glad that he had confessed his "crime" she promised to buy him a new glass and gave him an extra hug.

The lying pattern was broken and the many small "repair jobs" he did from now on didn't do any harm either. He learned to be more careful.

Paradoxical intention allows people to gain distance from themselves and look at their behavior patterns from the outside and with a sense of humor. It must not be used in such a manner that the clients feel the counselor is laughing at them, but to help them see, if only for a moment, how ridiculous their actions are. The technique breaks a behavior pattern, snaps it. The woman with the elevator phobia paradoxically intends to stop fearing a collapse and actually tries producing one; the husband, after having been tyrannized by his wife's threatened divorce, suddenly agrees and helps her pack; the father stops scolding his fighting sons and offers to take over the fighting himself. These unexpected reactions strengthen the clients' self-confidence undermined by their behavior. It is a relief to break out of the mesh of patterns, excessive emotions, and automatic reactions, and see the defiant power of the human spirit in action.

DEREFLECTION

Dereflection, the second specific logotherapeutic technique to help clients break their psychological shackles, counteracts the dangers of hyperreflection that traps victims so they see only their problems and nothing beyond. The problems dominate; no escape seems possible. The logical outcome of a pathologically magnified hyperreflection is suicide—the final exit when all thoughts revolve around a problem that seems unsolvable.

Human suffering is inevitable, but some are "unnecessary," brought on by the sufferer, often unintentional.

In my practice I am most often asked to help in cases of unnecessary suffering. A man, for whatever reason, begins to drink. He neglects his appearance, his acquaintances begin to withdraw. He becomes increasingly lonely which drives him closer to the bottle. He secretly drinks even in his office. His work suffers, he has conflicts with coworkers and his superior, and drowns his anger. He gets fired, undergoes a detoxification cure. After the cure he needs all his strength to resist the temptation of alcohol. But this is not enough. He also needs strength to look for new employment. He does not succeed and drowns his failure in drinking. His wife rebels—claiming that one stay in a detoxification clinic should be enough. After the second time she divorces him and now he is more isolated than ever: no friends, no work, no wife. His initial alcohol problem has quadrupled, wherever he turns nothing but problems. Under these circumstances a new beginning is almost hopeless, and if he stumbles now he is likely to stay down—a victim of alcohol. Yet his suffering has been unnecessary. With some will power and self-control he could have led a satisfying life among family, friends and coworkers. What he needed was something that was more important to him than the bottle, that would have motivated him to say "no" to the bottle, have occupied his thoughts more than the next beer. Needed was something that would have broken the deadly hyperreflection on alcohol and helped transcend it.

Dereflection leads clients to see the multitude of values that lie beyond their own weak selves. A man in danger of succumbing to alcoholism can be helped to shake his self-pity and regain the love of his partner or the trust of his supervisor, even if it requires great effort. The bottle shrinks to its true size, no longer magnified by hyperreflection.

Similarly, sleeplessness remains a problem as long as it is the center of attention. A woman who accepts the sleep her body grants and uses her sleepless hours to work at a task, or merely think about the task, is on her way to a cure. We must not make our happiness depend on a glass of wine, on undisturbed sleep, on the potency of our body or any other satisfaction of a need, because happiness cannot be captured that way. The best possible help for the happiness seeker is to dereflect—turning attention to a goal, a task, another person—and thus stop pursuing happiness, trying to satisfy needs directly. As Frankl put it, happiness *ensues* if it comes as a by-product of having found meaning.

Once I visited a home for severely retarded children in the company of two students. One remarked: "Terrible how these children suffer. I never could work here. I couldn't bear to watch them." The other said: "Well, if I knew there were not enough attendants available I wouldn't mind working here because every helping hand and every bit of love is needed." Both were compassionate, but the first thought about his own feelings, the other about the children. If we realize we are needed, our strength to tackle the task grows. If we concentrate on wondering whether our strength is sufficient, we attend to our weaknesses and feel frustrated.

Dereflection directs attention to a goal beyond the self. The dereflectory advice to persons suffering from psychogenic sexual dysfunction may be: "Don't observe your own potency, think of your partner." To the insomniac: "Don't worry about your sleep, use your time to write, paint, think about possible solutions to a problem that is bothering you." To the overweight person: "Forget sweets and your dieting, and keep on sewing that new beautiful slim-line dress."

It is difficult to get a person *not* to think about a troubling problem. The technique requires creative improvisations by the counselor, but it is worth the effort because it contains the key to the human spirit where the will to meaning can overcome the will to satisfy needs.

ATTITUDE MODULATION

Modulation of attitudes is therapeutic for clients facing unavoidable suffering. To avoid iatrogenic problems during the diagnostic phase counselors must consider in their expressions the relativity of truth. During the therapeutic phase counselors must show clients the relativity of values. They must enable a client suffering an inalterable situation, to see value in that situation. For instance, the counselor may discuss with a woman whose leg was amputated whether the value of human existence depends on the use of two legs, and explore opportunities for meaning despite, and even because of, her one-leggedness. Clients are often in despair because of a loss they cannot accept. Logotherapy suggests starting points for a best-possible bit of help in such situations. A modulation of attitudes may start with the consideration that "nothing (in the past) is irrecoverably lost but everything is irrevocably stored."

A recent widow may find consolation in the thought that not the length of a life made up the essential value of her husband but all those individual qualities that had made him worth her love—and that these are not wiped out by death.

Attitude is not determined by the situation but by the person. The first foggy fall days and the dropping of leaves are not bound to make us feel sad. We may associate fall with cozy evenings in front of the fire, the fragrance of pine needles. The observer alone determines by her attitude the emotional impact of her surroundings, her attitude in turn influences psychological health.

The therapist uses modulation with clients who face situations with attitudes so unhealthy or negative that mood, self-image, and therefore behavior is influenced. Attitude modulation is not dereflection but correction of reflection from a psychological unhealthy to a healthy attitude.

Case No. 10

A young mother complained bitterly about the work she had with her two small children. "I have no time for myself," she said. "Always I have to be after them and watch that they don't get into anything. I have to feed them, dress them, clean away their toys, wash mountains of laundry. To go shopping with the two is torture, and when they are finally in bed at night, I'm finished."

Here modulation of attitude has to take the form of near-shock, to shake up the mother. "Imagine," I told her, "the children get very sick and die. Then you would be free again of all your duties and could enjoy life..." "For heaven's sake!" cried the young mother. "I can't bear to even think about that! No, no. I'm glad my kids are healthy, even if they mean a lot of work. Perhaps I should not even talk about it, or God could hear me..."

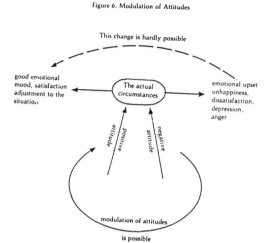

Figure 6. Modulation of Attitudes

Figure 6 shows that a situation of suffering can trigger good or bad moods, and that it is difficult in therapy to directly change the mood of clients. It is more promising to bring about change indirectly by modulating attitudes in a positive direction.

For instance, it is much harder to cheer up sad people than discuss the possibilities that the very situation which makes them sad may offer hidden meanings, or opportunities for inner growth and catharsis, chances to learn, to see suffering as the price for a value otherwise not attainable. They then see their suffering in a new light and meaninglessness is deleted from sadness.

Similarly, a mother may resent or enjoy the work with her children, depending on mood; it is hardly possible to change resentment to joy. But a modulation of attitude may open her to motherhood in a positive light, and indirectly lead to harmonious living with the children.

One widely held unhealthy attitude today is the conviction that, for one reason or another we simply are not able to do what we basically wish to do. Clients often quote reasons picked from popular psychology literature. Mr. A cannot love because his mother neglected him as a child; Mrs. B cannot help being grouchy in the morning because she has not had her second cup of coffee; the obese Mrs. C cannot pass a candy shop because she has a deep-seated compulsion to buy sweets; Mr. D cannot be assertive because he has an inferiority complex; Mrs. E cannot have a good marriage because her parents denied her the right kind of role-modeling.

All are able to overcome their blocks but don't know it because attitudes prevent them from trying. Thousands of people prove daily that a morning grouch can be friendly before coffee, phobics enter overcrowded supermarkets, people with disastrous childhoods are happily married, and nonassertive people are successful. Many clients do not try because they are convinced they will fail. They are caught in a vicious circle of negative expectations, of failures that seem to confirm expectations. If we do not try to overcome our weaknesses we won't overcome them; we never experienced a victory over them, so we succumb.

Negative attitude is intensified by affluence. In the West nowadays, we don't experience an outer necessity to overcome inner hurdles; we don't *have* to, so we think we *can't*. In times of deprivation people have no time to think about their inferiority complexes, anxieties, parents' neglect, or morning grouchiness. With survival at stake, phobics will enter crowded stores and people with unhappy childhoods will hold on to their partners, regardless of reasons why they "can't." Their actions prove that they *can* do what they would have thought impossible. Confidence grows with their experiences, the unfortunate attitude of "I can't" has no chance to develop. In this sense the child in affluent society is disadvantaged, and the percentage of the psychologically sick is correspondingly high.

The counselor seeks to change the unhealthy "I cannot because" to the healthy attitude of "I can in spite of." Many psychotherapies concentrate on exploring reasons why a client "cannot" rather than planning a course of action "in spite of" the handicaps. Logotherapists discuss "cannot reasons" to find out if factual limitations exist. They then lead the clients gradually and purposefully, toward "I don't have to take every nonsense from myself" (Frankl). They support the clients' defiant power to overcome their weaknesses. The method is usually successful because clients who have at least once experienced that "they can in spite of" are never again helpless victims of "inescapable" reasons that held them back. The door is open to the healthy attitude of "I can always change."

Case No. 11

An overweight woman casually remarked that she never could pass a certain candy store without indulging in sweets, and that she didn't even try. I interrupted her in the midst of our session and suggested putting on our coats and walking past that store. We could just as well continue our discussion on the street, I told her, and she could see for herself if she had will power to resist sweet temptations. And she resisted. Since then she walks purposely past that store to prove to herself that she can indeed resist.

Such an "aha" experience, even if it concerns a relatively insignificant episode, is a turning point. It helps clients develop a new attitude that will prompt them to conquer weakness or accept unchangeable fate courageously. They begin to understand that it is up to them to respond to the opportunities life offers. They have to do the responding—no one will do it for them. When they see that their actions are not automatic *re*actions but decisions they themselves make, they grow beyond their previous selves.

Case No. 12

A mother sought counseling because one of her daughters had serious problems. Her second daughter had been an unwanted child, was raised by her grandparents, later came back to live with her parents, was raped by her father, and then left the family. This daughter had developed into a healthy young woman with a good job and a satisfying relationship with a boy friend. The other daughter was a wanted child, raised by loving parents, given the best educational opportunities, had not been raped, yet was unstable and beset by problems.

This is reality not found in psychology textbooks. The theory of long-lasting traumas stands on shaky ground. A person exposed to severe traumas may lead a normal life while another growing up under positive circumstances goes astray. Every person responds to life in an individual way, influenced by past conditions but also free to defy them.

This "logotherapeutic credo" can help clients overcome unwanted behavior patterns even if they seem hopelessly fixed.

A modulation of attitudes can show people how to take charge of their lives instead of dangling helplessly on the strings of fate like puppets.

While specific logotherapeutic techniques put patients back on their feet, attitude modulation helps them stand securely under all conditions. It strengthens them against being toppled by unexpected blows of fate. These methods can be combined to accentuate the positive, to orient clients toward meaning and health regardless of the initial causes. It is important, however, that clients understand and accept the goals of therapy.

THE FOLLOW-UP PHASE

During the follow-up phase the counselor steers clients toward a middle course between excess stress and excess leisure.

Logotherapy considers both stress and leisure indispensable to mental health. Healthy stress is future oriented. It results from a reaching out beyond the present self toward a self to be attained, toward meanings to be found, tasks to be accomplished. Healthy leisure, on the other hand, issues from the past; it is a relaxation after a job well-done, a resting to gather strength before taking on the next task. A woman who puts all her efforts into achieving a much-desired goal will not be bothered by the stress her struggle causes and will resent interference. A man after having concluded an important task, relaxes happily warmed by the satisfaction it has brought, and will feel neither bored nor frustrated.

Problems arise when stress has no future and leisure no past; when people have to work hard without knowing what for, or when they live in leisure, without the effort that would make it meaningful. We can neither keep working without knowing why, nor live in perpetual leisure. Hans Selye who studied stress extensively, has called stress "the salt of life;" we cannot always eat salt, but we miss it if we don't have it.

Considerations of stress and leisure are important in the follow-up phase. If patients just recovered from illness are released into a situation of stress because they feel over-demanded, they may experience a relapse. On the other hand, if they are underdemanded and allowed too much leisure, they may hyperreflect again about problems they might have avoided, and so reactivate old symptoms.

There is no guarantee that clients are going to be released from therapy into ideal situations. They may find life more stressful than they can handle during recuperation, or they may be overprotected by well-meaning friends and relatives. However, logotherapy can strengthen the clients' spiritual muscles to prepare them for stresses that are bound to come sooner or later. Logotherapy can also help them acquire life goals to fill leisure time. Counselors accomplish these objectives by helping clients find individual meaning possibilities and by broadening base values.

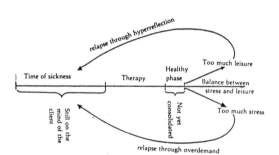

Figure 7. Stress and Leisure in the Follow-up Phase

Figure 7 illustrates why clients must be guided on a path between over- and underdemand. They have just managed to overcome problems, upsets, or sicknesses, and suffering still threatens. Follow-up treatment guides them on a balanced course between too much stress (causing a relapse through overdemand on a still weakened condition) and too much leisure (causing a relapse through hyperreflection).

DISCOVERING INDIVIDUAL MEANINGS

For the diagnostic phase I recommended the alternate diagnostic technique to counteract the danger of hyperreflection. During the follow-up, counselors can make good use of the additional information gained in previous phases about the clients' preferences and goals. These are stepping stones to mental stability and happiness.

One peril must be avoided: to discharge clients into a life reduced in meaning opportunities by sickness, without a replacement for losses. Even psychologically healthy people find it difficult to bear a reduction of life's contents. Those recovering from illness suffer even more.

Case No. 13

Mrs. S, a mother of two, had been hospitalized in a clinic three times for depression and general exhaustion. Every time she recovered but had a relapse. Before she was discharged the third time I was called in to talk to her.

During our entire discussion Mrs. S kept bringing up her children, recounting episodes from their lives, and hardly mentioned any other areas of interest. This was a warning signal. I had read in her medical report that the husband had sent the children to a boarding school to provide regular care for them and to relieve his wife from the strain of having the children around. From what Mrs. S had told me, the children had been central to her life, and now she would not be able to see them often. I was afraid that the emptiness of the house and lack of a task would create an existential vacuum in her. It would have required great strength of will and inner security to build up a new field of activity by herself—more than could be expected from a patient recovering from a depression. I suggested keeping her in the clinic until she had been given time to think about restructuring her life in the absence of her children. But the doctor was convinced she was well enough, and her husband, too, urged her to come home.

Three weeks later Mrs. S was brought back to the clinic. She had taken an overdose of sleeping pills and been saved in the nick of time. She had not been able to stand the stillness and emptiness of the house. Leisure and relaxation had not been sufficient to fill her life with meaning, especially since what had been most meaningful to her in the past had been removed.

After several sessions it became clear that Mrs. S had a fondness for animals second only to her love for her children. She succeeded in finding a job in the public zoo. She enjoyed her new work, and it was touching to hear her talk to the animals tenderly and watch her care for them individually. For her children it was a thrill that their mother's work gave them and their friends from the boarding school free access to proudly show them "their" zoo where their mother helped. One Sunday I want to visit Mrs. S at the zoo and saw from the distance how she laughed with the children. I went home convinced that the follow-up had been successful.

It is evident from many such examples that the entire therapy is jeopardized if the patient is discharged to a life lacking meaningful content. The follow-up requires that counselor and client go on a common search to discover a variety of ways to find meanings, to reconstruct existence, to appraise opportunities, and see the direction life is to take. This search also provides the best kind of dereflection, at a time when it is vital to forget sickness and remember it only in terms of achievement—to have overcome it.

Life offers many, often overlooked, meanings. Counselors do not create meanings, they merely elucidate them for clients to see and make them part of their thoughts and actions. Counselors draw attention to new life contents that may strengthen and give clients new incentives.

If Mrs. S, deep within, had not loved animals all along, she would not have found satisfaction in a job that gave new meaning to her life. I did not create her love for animals. I merely helped uncover it, to make her conscious of a potential at her disposal. This I was able to do because I had not restricted discussions to her depressive moods but talked to her as a woman with many healthy attributes that could bring satisfaction, and spread them out so she could choose one that suited her unique personality.

To elucidate individual meaning potentials is one of the two preconditions that help reduce recidivism. The other is a broadening of the base of the client's values.

BROADENING THE BASE OF VALUES

Some individual meaning goals cannot be realized. Mrs. S, for instance, might not have secured the job at the zoo, and that particular path would have been closed. But this failure would not have ended her fondness for animals and nature in general. No one could have prevented her from keeping a dog, from feeding birds in winter, or taking pictures of ducks in a pond. These activities might not have been enough to fill her day but this was not necessary. What she needed was enrichment of life, a feeling that she was useful.

People who see only one value to fill life, be it work, family, or material possessions, are in danger of losing and succumbing to despair. A variety, on the other hand—ideals, hobbies, interests and activities—provides a safety net that will break their "fall from great heights" when one of the values is lost.

Logotherapy points out the direct connection between mental health and the broad base of values that fill our lives. Logotherapy, like behavior therapy, has been accused of merely treating symptoms. Counselors, however, trying to enrich clients' value systems, are far removed from treating symptoms. They do not look for hidden whys and wherefores, for deep-seated disorders, drives, and deviations to be dragged into the daylight of consciousness; they push forward to the heights of ideas and ideals, elucidate the forces of the human spirit which alone assure mental health and productivity in the broadest sense, beyond all treatment of symptoms. Psycho-analytic and logotherapeutic procedures do more than "merely" treat symptoms, but clearly differ in two ways: In the direction from which they approach the symptoms, and in the sequence of treating them. Both direction and sequence are important in therapy; the direction for the self-understanding of the client, the sequence for the prevention of subsequent problems.

Figure 8. Approaches to Symptoms

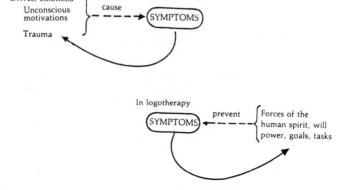

THE DIRECTION OF APPROACH

The counselor who looks for unconscious drives in interpreting symptoms creates a self-image of dependence in clients: they see themselves as not fully responsible for their actions because these are determined by their drives or the past. Their self-image is of persons dependent on outside influences. Therapy can make them conscious of and alleviate these influences, but they still see themselves as victims of drives and outside influences. All attempts to free themselves seem a hopeless struggle against impenetrable and ungovernable (i.e. unconscious) forces which dominate them against their will. Once clients have been steered in the direction of determinism it is difficult to change direction; this approach becomes part of their self-understanding and fosters nihilism and fatalism. Initiative is paralyzed, their readiness to take charge of their lives is weakened. They find it difficult to live according to their own values.

Counselors with a logotherapeutic world view lead clients to a different approach, to see a meaningful life, full of goals and tasks to be pursued in spite of adverse conditions. They reach their goals because the powers of the human spirit enable them to stand against their own weaknesses and drives. Counselors following this approach can supply the decisive turn toward mental health.

The clients' understanding of themselves and the world is oriented toward the positive. They see the whole range of possibilities and realize that it is up to them to actualize them. The logotherapeutically trained counselor presents a picture of a human being which gives hope and courage—the best gift that can be given to a client about to be discharged from treatment.

THE SEQUENCE OF TREATING SYMPTOMS

The sequence by which symptoms are reduced is important because each causes a chain reaction and new symptoms. Therapy is a race against time: namely, the time it takes to cure a symptom before it can cause new problems.

An hysterical condition, for instance, may cause a marriage to break up which, in turn, may lead to thoughts of suicide. This simple chain of three links makes it obvious that the time available for helping with the hysteria is limited to the time the marriage is intact, and that the marriage counseling, which becomes necessary, must conclude successfully before suicide tempts.

If counselors first look for causes of hysteria, the marriage may be in ruins before they are unearthed. By the time counselors are ready to use their findings to reduce the hysteria, the patient may have committed suicide. A dramatic example, to be sure, but it illustrates the importance of the sequence in which symptoms are treated. The counselor must first attack the dominant symptom to interrupt the fatal chain of events, even if they are not potentially as drastic as in the above example. Only then is there time for exploring possible causes or, more usefully, appealing to those powers in the client likely to prevent a recurrence of the symptoms.

In the follow-up, the best possible help is to anchor clients in a broad base of values. It is their responsibility to discover these values. They will be on the way to health if they can draw from a variety of values offered by their profession, family, hobbies, friendships, interests, fulfilling experiences, individual tasks, religious beliefs, even sufferings to be overcome. This range protects them from the egocentricity so widespread today, when even healthy people become asocial and isolated, and which overwhelms the sick through the terrible phenomenon of hyperreflection. Clients who pursue positive values and goals become spiritually alive, they grow beyond their present selves toward an inner fulfillment that lies beyond pleasure and pain, closer to "happiness" than anything else.

Not all treatment concludes on a note of inner growth, but the best possible help is to leave suffering people with the suggestion that they do have the possibility of shaping their lives responsibly, and filled with meaning, up to the last breath.

CHAPTER THREE

SUFFERING AND THE
QUESTION OF MEANING

Most schools of psychotherapy attempt to reduce human totality to a few rules. Logotherapy, on the other hand, tries to apply all its rules to the human totality. This requires that logotherapy enters areas which general psychotherapy considers beyond its province.

One area beyond our comprehension is unavoidab!e and unexplainable suffering. Logotherapy deals with the entire range of human problems, from those we can change to those we cannot. Its concern is to comfort, its goal is to find "the best possible help," its empathy is to patients who are led to realize that suffering is not meaningless.

A current illusion is that everything can be corrected. Overweight people diet, the weak take fitness training, the old go to rejuvenation centers. Shy people take assertiveness training, poor students concentration training and their parents a course in parenting. The magic word from behaviorist therapy, 'training,' has brought about a naive faith that everything disagreeable can be corrected. Training can achieve much but encountering the unavoidable is beyond it. Worse, it is seen as personal failure and injustice by Fate. This is a dangerous fallacy. A mechanistic psychotherapy is prone to prescribe training programs for any problem, and blame the participants if it is not solved. Few psychologies pay attention to the inevitable, to comfort where they cannot "cure."

We revolt against Fate but have forgotten how to accept it. I once attended a parent meeting to discuss the problem that English classes had to be dropped for half a year because all available teachers were sick. About a hundred parents were present, suggestions ranged from making petitions to the ministry of education, to demonstration marches through the city. Not one of the parents thought of offering to teach the children. My proposal to form learning groups in the afternoon with parents who know English met with only disbelief. No one was ready to do anything but protest. I was alarmed: how were the children to accept problems and find meaningful solutions if their parents were unable to do it?

Another illusion is our vague idea that everything can be bought. The "dance around the golden calf" ended in disaster— this has not changed in the twentieth century. Worse than the overvaluation of material things is devaluation of the immaterial, that which cannot be bought. A mother who receives from her grown son a costly bouquet of flowers, can buy it herself; but not the visit of her son. The feeling for this fine distinction has largely been lost.

People who have not learned to accept fate, who believe they can get almost everything for a price, are likely to despair when faced with unavoidable suffering. In such a crisis only three possibilities are open:

Faith and a belief in God,

Empathy and understanding from people around them,

Their own stable meaning fulfillment.

Faith in God has been shaken in many people's lives, and interpersonal support even more so. Thus, personal discovery of meaning remains the last decisive criterion whether or not we can surmount an inner crisis. People to whom we turn in such a crisis have shifted from minister and family to the psychotherapist.

In our loneliness we seek from strangers what we can no longer find in a firm faith or from people close to us. Psychotherapists, this "last hope," cannot afford to say "here I cannot help, this goes beyond my field of competence." Where scientific knowledge fails, humanity must take over. At the limits of understanding, empathy must find words.

Therapists who limit themselves to what is curable, practice their profession but fail in their vocation. In particular, my younger colleagues are satisfied with setting up therapy programs to correct and train. When, for instance, desperate parents call a psychological counseling center because their grown daughter has become involved in a dangerous cult, therapists are apt to say: "Your daughter obviously does not suffer and you no longer can influence a grown offspring, so therapy is pointless. If your daughter is in danger, you cannot stop her." It is true, a talk with the parents will not change the situation. Nevertheless, the question must be asked whether psychologists need to abandon parents to despair, or can support them in their suffering. The parents might see that, even in this crisis, meaning lies in a maturity their daughter would never gain without such experience.

Current psychological practice mostly disregards the dimension of the human spirit, as well as the area of pity. Modern psychologists know their profession but are not skilled in compassion. Compassion has little space in our industrialized world of neon signs and glittering shop windows. Who ever thinks of the thousands of people who commit suicide every year because they cannot bear their loneliness? They are often older people, forgotten, nobody wants to talk to, suffering, and no one listens. Does psychology exist only to determine questionable IQ's and to alter correctable behavior patterns? What a task it would be for psychology to help patients bear their suffering—mental, psychological, physical—when suffering is inevitable and Fate must be accepted!

If a young man has become a quadruplegic after a traffic accident medical help is of course most important. But after everything possible has been done, the patient faces the task of reconstructing his life and expectations. From now on, he is tied to a wheelchair. Psychology can contribute a great deal to this new orientation, if only by helping him find the strength to face his fate instead of being destroyed by it.

Self-pity is unhealthy, and psychotherapists must free clients from it and replace it by a compassion that opens new and positive attitudes toward their affliction. They need to know what positive attitudes are, and this leads to the question of meaning and to logotherapy.

Frankl has shown that success does not equate with meaning, nor failure with despair (see *Meaningful Living*, p. 11). He illustrates this in his famous "cross":

Figure 9. Relationship between Success and Meaning

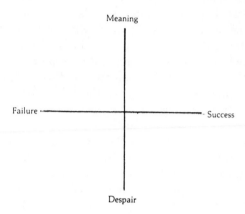

"Success" includes lucky breaks, wealth, health, good education, favorable living conditions, while "failure" includes bad breaks, poverty, ill health, unfavorable living conditions.

Today's existential frustration and crises of meaning lie in the quadrant between success and despair. People who are or could be well off but do not enjoy life, are bored, irritable and satiated, see no meaning in living. Statistical research has shown that in affluent societies 20% of the population fall into this group.

The success-despair quadrant is located in the lower right part of Figure 9. Despair caused by genuine suffering and misery lies between despair and failure (lower left). Every shift toward the upper part of the cross will contribute to psychological stability and inner happiness, regardless of where the person stands on the success-failure continuum.

To explore the connection between meaning and suffering, we look at the two upper quadrants, first the one between failure and meaning (upper left).

Logotherapeutic research has focused on efforts to transform suffering into human achievement through a positive attitude which gives strength and earns admiration. It starts with the assumption that the most severe suffering can be faced if meaning is perceived behind it. A mother, for instance, who runs into a burning home to save her child will not complain of her severe burns. The same woman may quarrel bitterly with fate if she suffered much lighter burns through an accident caused by an oversight.

Figure 10. Modulation of Attitudes in Situations of Failure & Success

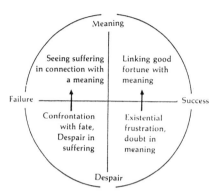

On the assumption that unavoidable suffering can be borne if a meaning can be seen in it, logotherapy tries to bring the suffering into connection with a meaning the patient can accept. This is not always easy.

Case No. 14

A 40-year old man came to see me and asked if I could find a good home for his infant, "if need be." When I inquired what he meant by "if need be," he broke down, sobbing. He told me that his wife had inoperable cancer, and the physicians had expected her to die before the child was born. As by a miracle the baby was born healthy.

I promised the man to look out for a good home, and he asked if I would tell this to his wife, too, because she too worried about the child's future. I asked them to meet me the next day.

This case illustrates how insignificant the question of competency becomes in the face of the unavoidable. Psychologists do not find homes for infants—but I was not asked as a psychologist. I was challenged as a human being.

The next day I asked them to tell me about their life together. They were married six years, had always been close, more so since the wife's illness. The child was an unexpected gift that had stirred their emotions deeply, especially since it turned out so unexpectedly well.

When they finished, there was a pause. Then I told them something like this: "Mr. and Mrs. X, I congratulate you both heartily. You have shown in your short shared life so much mutual love and courage as very few couples, even after 30 or 40 years of marriage experience. Hundreds of married couples come to our counseling center, and what I hear are trivial disputes, selfishness, and mutual distrust. Only rarely will two people relate so happily as you have. This is something to be proud of, because what matters is not how long two people live together but how intensely they fill their lives with mutual respect and love. If I add the hours of harmony in many of the marriages where both partners have the good fortune to live a long life, the total hours of harmony would hardly approach the six years you were able to live happily together. No one can take away those past years and you deserve to be congratulated."

The husband's eyes were moist, and the wife reached out for my hand. "I am not unhappy about the fate that will separate us soon," she said, "I'm worried about my husband. I am afraid he may lose his hold, when he is alone." "But, Mrs. X, "I replied. "You do leave him a hold on life, there is hardly a stronger kind—a task for which he is responsible: the child of your love. No one who is aware of a task which he knows he has to fulfill, will lose his grip, he will even find strength to help others. Your husband will remain strong, even when you are no longer with him, strong enough to support the child and to bring it up well." Here the husband jumped to his feet, knelt before his wife and solemnly promised to find the strength to bring up the child as long as it needed his care. They left our counseling center serenely and confidently, though no circumstances had changed.

What was helpful in this logotherapeutic discourse was not "comfort"—there can hardly be comfort for a person facing death. Here the important thing was finding some meaning connected with the two questions weighing on them. Why did their happy togetherness have to end so suddenly, and what would happen after the wife's death? If a short married life had brought more happy hours than many a long marriage, then the number of hours and years is less important than content. The six happy years retain their meaning even when abruptly ended. The woman knows she has left the child to her husband, a task and a support to help him over his sorrow: the birth of the child before her death is a powerful legacy of their mutual love, transcending death. The tragedy of the inevitable is softened by the awareness of a fulfilled life.

Not every case deals with helping the dying, of course. Often people must continue to live, with suffering.

Case No. 15

A mother came to the counseling center without an appointment, with a diminutive somewhat ill-proportioned girl. "Do you have a worry with the young lady?" I asked her unsuspectingly. The girl grabbed an ashtray and threw it against the wall. "I'm not a young lady!" she yelled. I asked the mother to remain in the waiting room and told the girl to sit down. "It's you who have a great worry," I said. "We'll share it like sisters. If you want to keep part of it to yourself, that's all right. But the part you want to share, please tell me, and we will see what we can do."

What she told me was heart-rending. She was 18 years old, but she stopped growing although she had undergone an operation, a spinal puncture and several stays in hospitals. The doctors suspected that something was wrong with her hypophysis. She tired easily, had little immunity against sickness, and in general was fed up being mistaken for a child. School, too, was a problem; mother tried to help her graduate from high school through private lessons, but frequent illness prevented this as well as normal school attendance. After she had poured out her heart, I called in the mother who could not add anything except that she did not know how her daughter could live with her abnormality.

I turned to the daughter. "I have to apologize that I mistook you for a child," I said. "But I couldn't know your real age. This is also true for others. I hope you will learn to forgive them because no one is guilty if it is not done on purpose.

"But now I'd like to ask you something. If your first impression of a person changes after you get to know her, is it better if the first impression is not so great and you discover the true qualities of the person later, or is it better if the first impression is good and the disappointment comes afterwards?"

"No," said the girl. "It is better if a person has better qualities than appears at first."

"You see," I went on. "That's what happens with you. If you had the body of a mature young woman and the mind of a child, people would see you as a grown up and be disappointed that you are mentally immature. You first look like a child but it soon becomes evident that you are a grown-up young woman with a mature and sharp mind. You are not able to give the first impression of an adult, but your second impression is vastly better; it will come as a surprise to people you meet. Just because people will make a mistake in the beginning, you will rise considerably in their respect when they know you better. When I, for instance, meet someone I'll have to think up something special at the second meeting if I want to improve their first impression. You can do this without any effort." The girl laughed and said: "That's true, I can always surprise people when they speak to me as to a child and I answer them with a few sophisticated words."

The young woman realized during our talk that her ability to surprise people lay in the false impression she first gave. This made her frustration more bearable; she even saw a positive aspect in anticipating the surprise of strangers.

We expanded this line of thought. She could surprise others more if she would increase her vocabulary and knowledge. Wisdom and well-founded information, coming from a seemingly twelve-year old, were bound to impress people, even after the mystery cleared up. The girl's spirits picked up when she thought of the acceptance and recognition she would receive, because up to now she always felt excluded.

Together with the mother we explored the educational possibilities. We finally decided to try correspondence courses which sent materials to students at certain intervals and corrected the written exercises. By this method, periods of sickness and weakness would not endanger her educational progress. When she said goodbye the girl remarked with a smile that I could now address her as "young lady." I would not be making fun of her; she would really feel like a young lady. A few days later a little package arrived by mail, containing an ashtray and a greeting.

Here, too, the glimpse of a meaning helped find a positive attitude to an unalterable situation. The help we can give often is based on small-seeming matters, and we must not forget that despair is also often based on a small particular.

Facing the inevitable, believing there is no meaning in anything, we walk on thin ice. A minor shift in attitude brings us to firmer ground.

If we can continue modulating attitudes with a bit of humor, a smile, and wider view, stability becomes attainable. The true heroes of life are not the triumphant victors but the defeated who find a ray of hope. Clients who can reconcile themselves to weakness in a positive and sometimes even humorous manner, show what people are capable of.

Logotherapy considers positive attitudes toward inevitable fate so important that they hold a special place among human values. Frankl sees three values that help us lead a meaningful life: Creative values (what we do physically and mentally), experiential values (what we experience in nature, art, human relationships), and also attitudinal values (facing the inevitable). We may face it angrily or calmly, heroically or wailing, be an admirable or a horrible example for others. Here lies the opportunity of suffering persons to see meaning. In the manner we bear our suffering we determine its value. Both case histories place in the upper left quadrant of Figure 9. Fate forced these persons into "failure" but attitudinal values changed suffering into achievement.

Attitudinal values can also be attained in the upper right quadrant of Figure 9. Positive attitudes can be important in situations of good luck and success.

Imagine two drivers on a highway—both are in the same situation. Suddenly the first driver skids into a ditch. He is unhurt but his car is a total loss. The situation has changed: one driver has lost his car, the other can continue driving.

On the horizontal continuum, the first driver is on the side of "failure" (misfortune), the second on the side of "success" (good fortune). Both situations are determined by "Fate," beyond personal control. In the first case suffering is in the foreground, in the second good fortune is darkened by awareness that the other has suffered; here suffering is in the background.

Of course, our own suffering concerns us more than that of others. Nevertheless, affluent times have prompted people with "good fortune" to find meaning by attitudinal changes. The young generation of our time, from affluent families, see meaning in demonstrations, sometimes even getting arrested for causes of others whose fate contrasts sharply with their own.

In the case of the two drivers, the first is affected by his own suffering, the second by the other's misfortune darkening his own situation. The first is challenged to find a positive attitude to what happened, for instance to learn from the accident, to see the damage as a sort of apprenticeship fee. This links the accident with meaning and helps him accept it.

The second driver, in this contrasting situation, is also challenged to find a positive attitude by finding a link to meaning. His car is intact and he can use it to take the other to the police or a hospital. He is well, and can help the other get over his shock and comfort him. A positive attitude to our own good fortune and success always leads to responsible action toward others.

If the first driver became inconsolable over the loss of his car to the point of suicide , or if the second driver went on without trying to help, these negative and dangerous attitudes would demonstrate a lack of responsibility and override meanings and values inherent in such situations.

The best attitude toward unavoidable suffering focuses on the concept of "heroism," the best attitude in good fortune focuses on the concept of "humanism." Suffering persons must face a fate that might have been more fortunate. Those blessed by good fortune must attend to other people's fate which could have been theirs.

Facing one's own suffering does not always have precedence. In the conflict between the races, for instance, it would be up to the whites (on the side of "success") to find a positive attitude toward blacks as equals, before the blacks (on the side of "failure") can be expected to find positive attitudes in being black in a white society.

Realizing both these attitudinal values helps us find meaning in our own lives and also strongly affects others. An heroic attitude to our own suffering indirectly helps others through example. Selfless kindness to others helps directly. Positive attitudes in situations of suffering earn admiration, and those in situations of good fortune earn gratitude.

I term the modulation of attitudes in the success-meaning quadrant of Figure 10 a "generalized attitudinal value." Though Frankl does not use this term, I believe I am within the framework of logotherapy in adding to the meaning of suffering the meaning of helping. Only those can help who are in a position to help: the rich can support the poor, the healthy nurse the sick, the intelligent guide the uneducated, the strong support the weak.

Physicians and psychologists are in the position of the second driver. They must find meaningful and responsible attitudes toward their clients by perceiving them not only as people who are sick, shipwrecked, or unstable but as human beings whose suffering are also their concern.

Many people seek counseling because they cannot cope with suffering. However, some people who "cannot cope with their good fortune" also need help. Here are two examples.

Case No. 16

A woman, around 30, had a thorough organic checkup because she felt moody and apathetic. When the doctor told her that the examination showed her to be in perfect physical condition, she reacted unexpectedly. If she was healthy and no one could help her, she burst out, she might as well commit suicide. The doctor sent her to our counseling center.

The woman could not give any reason for her negative attitude. "I'm well off," she said, "but I don't enjoy living." "Were you always well off?" I asked. She thought a while, then told me that she had to interrupt high school when her parents divorced, found minor employment, been ambitious and worked hard in evening classes to attain a high school diploma. She entered the civil service, worked conscientiously and reached the highest level available, tenure with full pension.

"Was this the time when your apathy began?" I asked. She admitted that this could be so. "Then I think I know what you need," I ventured. "You need a goal. All your life you have been ambitious, and now suddenly you've reached your goal and cannot advance. But you have too much mental energy to stand still, you need challenges, new areas of activity. To be well off is not enough, standing still does not satisfy human nature." The woman had listened attentively and was no longer uninterested. "You are right," she said. "What I need is a goal. Now that you've said it, I know it is true. And here I thought you will analyze my entire childhood and trace my difficulties back to the divorce of my parents . . ." We both laughed, and the ice was broken.

It was difficult to find a goal for a woman who had reached the peak of her career. Just the knowledge that she could not be fired put the brakes on motivation—what meaning was there if the outcome was the same whether she worked well or not?

This was the opportunity for realizing a generalized attitudinal value. "You are standing on top of a mountain and look into the valley," I said, "but the view below depresses you, you are used to looking up. Others wander about the foot of the mountain and cannot find the way up. Would you be willing to go down and guide them up? To know that you are important for others would give you satisfaction, and your eyes would be turned upward again."

She understood immediately. "I know what you are telling me," she said. "I've all this time thought of myself and overlooked others." She got up. "I'll come again," she promised. "You'll be satisfied with me."

She did come again, tired but radiant and full of plans. She had offered, in the ministry where she worked, a free course for beginners as preparation for the civil service test, and received such a positive response that she hardly knew how to handle the task. She now considered offering similar courses in adult education. "Thank God I have tenure," she smiled, "or I would be afraid this volunteer work would make me neglect my job and I'd be fired." And then she added, "You were right. I have a goal, and I have learned that others have to be included if our activities are to have meaning."

This woman could be dismissed from the counseling center with confidence. Her apathy and depression were gone.

I was lucky in this case because it is not often that a patient understands and cooperates in therapy as willingly as she did. To include others in one's own good fortune, to give this good fortune a deeper meaning and thus get well—this often meets with resistance.

Case No. 17

A student spent the whole hour in telling me about his really remarkable successes. His grade average, fast advances, the well-paying part-time job which enabled him to live in affluence were the center of his thinking. He would make a brilliant career.

Eventually I asked him why he had come to me. He looked at me in disappointment. "You too," he mumbled, "You too don't want to hear what I have done? You too...well, I might as well go."

I asked him to stay. I realized what had brought him to a psychotherapeutic clinic. He needed an audience. There he was, with his supergrades, proud and isolated by his successes, quite incapable of linking his theoretical peak position with practical meaning.

I tried for hours to make him realize that his intelligence and knowledge would only be fruitful if he would apply them meaningfully, either in work with a goal, or to inspire and help others whose reaction would be meaningful to him. The second alternative, especially, would build bridges with others which he so urgently needed. "You are looking for listeners," I told him. "But what you really need are people who look to you and your talents, and thus let you know what your superachievements are good for." "I don't need the thanks of others," he replied. "The others should make their own efforts, then they will be as successful as I am. Each person for himself."

This unhealthy attitude toward his own achievements and successes blocked his meaning orientation and poisoned his potentially happy life. He kept coming back with the same resistance so that the therapy slowly stagnated.

One day I had an interesting talk with a Peace Corps worker who had been in South America. He told me what experts were needed and what problems had to be solved. I invited the student to join us. The Peace Corps worker told us what enormous demands were placed on the teachers, technicians, engineers, craftsmen, physicians, and social workers. Every day they had to face new situations, new difficulties, had constantly to think of new ideas to achieve something in the face of the mistrust of the population, problems of distribution, climatic difficulties, political upheavals, and sanitary dangers. The student, on his part, told about his studies and his vague feeling of frustration, whereupon the Peace Corps worker called out: "Boy, do we need people like you! Take your exam and join us, then you can use your keen mind, and when you'll labor all day you'll at least know what you are living for!"

After this session I didn't hear from the student for a long time. I gave him another appointment but he called to cancel it.

He had no time, he said, he had started to study Portuguese, it was just before his exam, and he did not need counseling. I didn't ask questions but from this study of Portuguese I drew conclusions, and was glad he reacted so positively to being needed by others, and linking his achievements with a meaningful goal.

Success for its own sake is no success, happiness as an end in itself is not happiness. Success and happiness must be shared with others if they are to play a satisfactory role in a person's psychic health. Figure 11 indicates that today's meaning crisis (lower right) is directly affected by the general attitude in our affluent society not to help others (upper right). Existential frustration and doubts in the meaning of life can be swept aside by opening ourselves to others.

Figure 11. Sociological Trend in Today's Search for Meaning

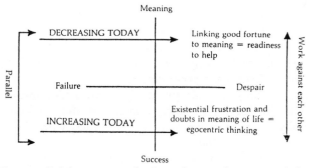

The parallel between today's widespread existential frustration and the frightening egocentricity and unconcern about others show that the feeling of meaninglessness and concern for others work against each other. Courage in suffering works against despair, concern for others works against meaninglessness—these relationships have to become part of our psychotherapeutic concepts if we are not to stop at surface corrections.

The following case history shows that in decisive therapeutic moments concern for others can be activated against the meaninglessness in one's own life.

Case No. 18

A middle-aged woman made several attempts at suicide. She suffered from an endogenous depression that came at intervals. During the depressive phase she took medication, the only way to reduce symptoms. She became addicted to her medication and took increasing amounts for it to be effective, eventually such a large quantity that she could not afford to buy it.

Medication stopped, the depression returned in full force, she saw no other way out and took an overdose of sleeping pills.

Her husband was keeping close watch and had been able to save her in time. It starts with hospitalization, her depressive phase ends, she has new hope until after a few months another depressive phase drives her to more medication. Her despair is less from relapses than feeling that life is meaningless because she cannot break the vicious cycle.

Indeed, there was little she could do: the endogenous phases and her addiction were so closely linked and so dependent on her malfunctioning organism that all therapy failed. I decided to fight for one thing: a reduction of the danger of suicide.

Fragment of the therapeutic dialogue:

Mrs. X: Why don't they let me die? What's the purpose of it all? That's no life, always this sadness, with no way out except a few pills that make everything seem even more hopeless.

E. L.: Mrs. X, suppose you suddenly got the idea to live in Hamburg instead of in Munich. Would you pack your suitcases, say goodbye, and move?

Mrs. X: (surprised) I—no, my son goes to school here, my husband works here... I'm not alone in the world!

E. L.: That's right, Mrs. X, that's the key sentence which you should never forget, whatever happens. You are not alone in the world. Your life is part of the basis of existence for other people around you. That's why you wouldn't move to Hamburg, and that's why you can't throw away your life, even if it sometimes seems to make little sense. At least it has a lot of meaning for your family. You are not alone in the world... Will you take your own sentence to heart?

Mrs. X: To tell you the truth, I don't think of my family when I'm down.

E. L.: Your own problems are the center of your thoughts. You want to get rid of your problems and not think of those your "solution" creates for others, especially those close to you. Try to reverse your thinking, and by your own free will take on the suffering problems to save others from having them.

Mrs. X: You want me to take my problems willingly?

E. L.:   Look at it this way, Mrs. X. If your life seems
         meaningless when you are down, but you decide to
         bear it patiently for the sake of your son who needs a
         mother and for the sake of your husband who would
         suffer from your suicide, then your life no longer is
         meaningless. Then you'll know why and for whom you
         live. Does that make sense?

Mrs. X: (thoughtfully) I think so. You are talking about my
         responsibility to my family. There I really have fallen
         short.

E. L.:   Your family is suffering, too. Your husband and your
         son cannot diminish your suffering, but you can
         diminish theirs!

Mrs. X: That's true. Strange, in the hospital I always thought
         how wretched I was, not even allowed to die. I am
         beginning to see that others, innocent people, suffer
         because of me. My husband is desperate...I must not
         do it again. I'll try at least this much in my life, to spare
         my family suffering.

Not every psychological distress can be therapeutically
corrected. Some must simply be borne, and the more we know a
"what for" the more we can bear it. We must perceive a reason,
a person we care for, a task to perform, something worth
suffering for. Here a therapeutic method meets an ancient ethical
principle because, as my patient understood, we are "not alone
in this world," and our own wellbeing cannot be our main
purpose in life. On the contrary, wellbeing in a vacuum,
separated from interpersonal relationships, is nothing.

Two special cases of suffering are old age and what I would
call "noetic dissonance."

Old age is not suffering in the strict sense but a natural part
of life. But the illusion that everything can be bought with
money has prompted ingenious techniques designed to post-
pone, or at least hide, old age. This only shocks and destabilizes
people when they are finally confronted with the inescapable
fact that, despite all efforts to the contrary, they are old.

People revolt against the fate of old age, and our society,
instead of making old age attractive, supports this revolt partly
for economic gains, until capitulation becomes catastrophe.

Complexes can be manufactured. It is risky to stereotype
women over 50 on television as depressed and unfulfilled

because they are not in full bloom of the love cycle. And it isn't helpful if grandpa is presented as out of touch, shaking his head over the loose morals of his grandchildren.

Figure 12. Shift in Capacities According to Age

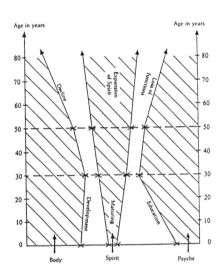

Actually, old age is remarkable for the chance to expand the spirit which previous life phases do not offer to that extent. Figure 12 was suggested by Kazimierz Popielski, professor at the University of Lublin, Poland.

He points out that the newly born is physically well developed but the capacity of the spirit exists only as potential. During the first 30 years all dimensions expand, during the next 20 they remain fairly constant, though body and psyche slowly decline, while the spirit keeps broadening even after age 50 if not prevented by circumstances or illness. The less latitude in the body and psyche, the more important are gains in spiritual development that can remain active into very old age.

These are the gifts of old age: strength of spirit based on a mature philosophy of life, a rich meaning orientation based on a lifelong search and struggle, a secure value structure built by personal experiences, and the memory of an abundant and unique life. These are the quiet blessings of the late years, unfortunately often lost in today's unhealthy attitudes toward old age.

We cannot convince older clients to look for goals in life and make efforts to reach them. Most goals have been attained, or are unattainable; the lifespan remaining is uncertain. We have to make them aware of the treasures they have accumulated in their spiritual dimension, and divert their attention from physical decline and psychological functional losses (in memory, quickness of comprehension, flexibility of thought, assimilation of new impressions), toward a spiritual growth ever available. Knowing there are still possibilities to expand capacities insures the psychic health of the aging as it cancels out feelings of final limits. Young people still shaping their lives could learn from the mature if they would not look down in arrogance or pity on those who know life longer and are closer to their final destination.

Older clients need awareness that they have much to give, and the therapists, if the occasion arises, may well turn the situation around and ask for help—sometimes this is enough to elucidate new meaning and thus take the sting from suffering.

Life is self-regulating, and we can only help a little. We can and must not do more because no one knows what would happen if we could completely take over the regulating.

The second special case of suffering concerns "noetic dissonance," referring to the "cognitive dissonance" of Leon Festinger.

Existential frustration, as shown, is characterized by inner emptiness, lack of adequate goals, and motivation to reach them. But it can happen that goals and motivation are present but external circumstances interfere. "Cognitive dissonance" takes place when we have made a choice which in retrospect turns out to be questionable. "Noetic dissonance" refers to a choice that suddenly turns out to be unfeasible. These persons have a meaning-and-goal orientation, they know what they want, but their hands are tied and they watch helplessly as their chances evaporate. The stronger the inner meaning orientation, the stronger the "noetic dissonance" after the disappointment, ending in unavoidable suffering. To go back to previous cases:

What would happen if the child of the cancer victim died, if the growth-retarded woman could not complete correspondence courses, the civil servant were not permitted to give extra courses, the student not accepted in the Peace Corps, or the husband of the depressive woman divorced her?

Some goals can be replaced, others not. Also, not everyone has the flexibility to switch goals. The psychotherapist can try to arouse interest in new and perhaps similar goals, but there are limits. Sometimes it is possible to shift the emphasis within the three values: from creative values of actions, now limited by Fate, to contemplative experiential values or, if these are not feasible, to greater emphasis on attitudinal values. Gradual guidance to a new basic attitude to life can be more effective than a feverish search for substitute goals which cannot replace what was lost. We may suggest that clients accept, with the loss of a goal, a restructuring of the entire concept of their lives. This approach can better engage their cooperation than attempts to belittle lost goals or make them sound replaceable. In despair patients are likely to defend lost goals and become fixated on them.

The loss of an important life goal must not be hushed up either, or it will remain unexpressed behind every word and thought. It *must* be integrated in a meaning content. Never is meaning so much in the minds of people as after a severe loss. Patients whose life goals have gone astray will openly confront the psychotherapist with the question: "What meaning is left in my life?" We cannot evade answering, or claim that we are not the right people to consult.

The psychologist *must* find an answer, the psychotherapist *must* be able to face the client as openly as the answer is asked. A goal does not represent the meaning of life, and the loss of a goal does not spell meaninglessness. A goal may be reachable or not, both possibilities were once present but the meaning of life is always available.

If we could reach *the* meaning of life, any living beyond would be meaningless. Beyond reach, it would have no significance for us. The meaning of life is neither reachable nor unreachable, not repeatable or replaceable. The meaning of life lies in its pursuit. We may project meaning to something within us or in the outside world but it is actually the projection of human search and human will.

CHAPTER FOUR

GUILT AND THE QUESTION OF MEANING

Case No. 19

Anna, a guest worker in Germany, was sentenced to two years in prison and loss of custody of her child. She confessed to having burned her four-year old Joseph with a flat iron. In view of her immaturity and psychological instability the judge put the girl on probation on condition that she take psychiatric treatment for four years.

The guardian of the child asked me at that time to treat the mother while little Joseph was cared for in a foster home. I still have two and a half years to help the mother become a responsible member of society, keep her violent temper in check, normalize her relationship to her family, and learn from her guilt instead of being crushed by it. No easy task and a great responsibility because there is no guarantee that, in spite of all psychological help, she will not repeat the deed, either on the child during visits or on others, perhaps even after a long time. A person who sadistically tortures a victim might do it again.

Guilt, a great suffering, is all the more painful because it is brought on by ourselves. Countless tragedies on the stage have dealt with it because it sums up *the* human tragedy in one word. Animals suffer and die, only humans feel guilt, the stigma after the "expulsion from Paradise."

Psychotherapy has long been concerned with the problem of guilt. Almost all research focuses on how much is to be allocated to the individual, and how much to the environment, past and present. Some psychologists tend to free the individual of *all* guilt, with the consequence that every action by a person is seen as "caused by others."

In our case they may say it was not Anna's fault to have fits of anger because her mother spoiled her as a little child while her father was over-strict, the model of an ill-tempered parent. This view regards the grandparents of the child, not the mother, to be at fault.

Such considerations, however, are specious. If our actions are really so strongly influenced by others, then they, in turn, were determined by others, so every atrocity reveals only a chain of innocent people who pass on the guilt. This old deterministic principle defeats itself: if there is human guilt, it exists for everyone; if none, it exists for no one.

It is therefore not true (as widely believed) that the less guilt is borne by the individual, the more it is borne by others, and vice versa. The valid relationship is rather:

The less guilt is borne by the individual, the less it is borne by others, and:

The more guilt is borne by the individual the more it is borne by others.

If we consider Anna guilty because she could have controlled her anger enough not to hurt her child, we also acknowledge the guilt of the child's grandparents, not because of child abuse but because they brought up Anna the wrong way presenting conflicting role models.

More important than wrangling about guilt or no guilt is what meaningful and positive aspects can be found in one's own guilt (or even in the guilt of others). Here psychology is silent: if no guilt, there can be no positive aspects of guilt.

We have a paradox: psychologists who acquit persons from guilt to spare them negative consequences (punishment), unwittingly take away the positive potentials of guilt. Those acquitted have to live with their deed and their feelings about it. "Psychological excuses" don't calm the conscience, the very dependencies used to exonerate them make them feel like dependent children.

People in psychology should have the courage to recognize guilt as an essential part of human life which, like any other part, has meaning. The most obvious is to make amends and, where this is not possible, to learn from one's guilt so the wrong is not repeated. There are many ways to deal with guilt as long as it is not downplayed by denying it. We deal with guilt by admitting it, by changing into a "new person" who has learned his lesson.

Anna still has not admitted her guilt. She insists that her confession at the trial was made under duress. Joseph, she claims, had fallen on a hot stove. I am not her judge and do not have to extract the truth from her: I am certain that some day she'll tell me everything. Meanwhile she has told me enough about events which made her feel guilty and are a starting point for our work: to deal with her hysterical outbursts, childish defiance, impulsive recklessness, confused life planning, and harmful overreactions.

We did not spend much time in exploring where all this behavior came from. What good is it to know what mistakes her parents committed? Mistakes were made, especially by the mother who spoiled her daughter and contributed to her "hysterical character." It is a strange phenomenon that spoiled children become "addicted" to claiming more and more attention. They are used to getting their way, and demand affection far beyond what is normal. It is not necessarily true that children who crave attention do so because they didn't get enough affection from their parents. Sometimes the contrary is the case: too much attention received breeds a craving that can never be satisfied and the child's character development is endangered as a result.

In our case mistakes were made by spoiling Anna, but I am wary about dwelling on them. The young woman spends almost every vacation in her home country with her parents who love her and stuck to her even during the trial. I am not going to destroy that anchor by making mother or father the scapegoat. I have more important things to do than dig up mistakes from the past: the present has to be used, the future shaped.

Early in this book I spoke of the psychotherapist's delicate task to walk the ridge between two abysses, with an occasional glance down.

A look at Anna's past is such a glance. It lures us into a bottomless pit. I am convinced that I could spend the entire four years allotted to me to explore the depth of the girl's past. Entangled in the intricacies of various depth interpretations I may not find access to the heights of free human decision-making. Perhaps I would even be tempted to agree that Anna had no other choice than to hurt her child and thus to accept her self-image as a human puppet. But logotherapy has taught me to resist this temptation—for the sake of the patient.

And so I turned my attention to Anna's recent past and to the present.

I have used the term "hysterical character," a phrase that needs to be clarified. In everyday use the word "hysterical" implies repugnant behavior, and "character" unalterable characteristics we are born with. But there are also hysteric types who are lovable, displaying amazing changes in character.

Frankl lists three essential character traits for hysterics: they are liars—everything in them is exaggerated, untrue; they are egocentric, use every means to reach their goal; and they are calculating, wanting to be the center of attention.

These characteristics enable clever hysterics to cast themselves in positive roles if this serves their purpose: they may *seem* to be compassionate, understanding, helpful, and ready to make sacrifices. They know exactly the right moment for the big scene, to get the greatest mileage out of their performances. They use their bodies for fainting spells, fits of crying, screams of pain, fever, weakness, vomiting, paralyzed apathy. The more they succeed the more they are used, so that hysterical persons can keep whole families in suspense until their every wish is granted lest there be new "attacks."

From calculated egoism to blackmail is a small step and part of the hysteric repertoire. Hysterics threaten and even attempt suicide to arouse sympathy in even the most resisting onlooker.

Hysteria can be cured, but not by going into its history. Patients enjoy this immensely because it makes them the center of attention. Scientific research shows that hysterics reproduce childhood events that comply with expectations of the various therapeutic schools—sexual traumas for psychoanalysts, inferiority complexes for individual psychologists, archetypal symbols for Jungians, and so on. Hysteria can be cured only through re-education, by stimulating inner maturation: the patients' character needs to be remodeled.

One approach is to ignore the performance, but this only increases hysterical efforts. It is extremely difficult for people close to hysterics to remain firm in the face of simulated mental and physical breakdowns. Also, ignoring the threats can have dangerous consequences because arteries cut only to shock a family member often lead to death.

The family of the patient finds it difficult not to show concern because it is so hard to distinguish what is genuine. It is too much to ask of persons close to an hysteric to remain emotionally detached. This is the devilish part of the problem: it keeps going because if hysterical attacks attain their purpose they are repeated, and this fixates patients in their pattern.

Since it is difficult to prevent hysterical performances from having calculated effects, hysterics must learn to give up performances, gratifications notwithstanding. Learning to give up something helps a maturing process that will soften egocentricity. To cure means to motivate hysterics to give up something experienced as valuable.

A warning: It is tempting but dangerous to quickly "diagnose" other people as "hysterics." I myself am cautious because many disorders with elements of hysteria are covered up by desirable character features, resulting in a quite different personality picture. No person can be completely typified, everyone is unique and can be typified only to a certain point.

Our young mother had all the symptoms of hysteria but we must not judge her too harshly. Her guilt and the loss of custody of her child are punishment enough. It is my task to help her. Hysterics, as noted, can be cured by reshaping character, by motivating them to "give up" something. If I can help Anna toward maturity, then the episode of child abuse is not entirely without meaning. It is a bitter but necessary step toward a development which could result in many benefits. Every crisis stimulates major advances in a person's development, and the experience of heavy guilt often is the starting point of a maturation which otherwise would not have taken place. That little Joseph had to suffer so his mother could mature is, of course, tragic but this is not quite the interpretation to hold to. One might see it this way: Anna's immaturity would have caused much suffering had it not been stopped by the severe and visible suffering of the child. This incident brought the mother to her senses and led to therapy that could help her mature.

Logotherapy, based on the assumption that life has meaning under all circumstances, provides guidelines toward a clear therapeutic goal that can be reached in cooperation with the patient even in "hopeless" cases. It may not always be possible to reach this goal but as therapist I give it prime consideration.

In my work with Anna I am still far from our goal but we are on our way. It leads to many bitter realizations; she keeps stumbling and reaching for my hand. She still cannot talk about the maltreatment of the child but she talks a lot about her lacking rapport with him. Her story is familiar. She came to Germany to earn money, very young, not knowing the language. The lures of the big city tempted her, she became pregnant hardly knowing the father of the child. When she gave birth she had no idea what would happen next, she had no plans. She was persuaded to give up the baby for adoption but in an "hysterical" scene she rescinded her consent and the boy went to a series of foster homes, with differing styles of childrearing. Anna visited the boy, brought him small gifts but remained a stranger. She could not manage her money, found it hard to pay the foster parents, was unstable and insecure. She was lucky to meet a simple man who liked children, married her, and took in the boy. They had a second and much wanted child, and this could have been a happy ending but it was not to be. The shades of her past provoked her "hysterical character."

A child is no object one picks up and brings home to own. The rapport with a child must be won slowly, patiently, and with steady love. Mothers who have been separated from their infants for a long time require enormous inner strength to put aside their own wishes and establish, step by step, a basis for mutual trust. Without a strong relationship with the mother, the child resists all orders, becomes aggressive, obstinate, spiteful, challenging the mother who is likely to become overly strict. If the mother remains calm and realizes that the child's behavior is caused by the changed situation, her patience will be rewarded because children adjust pretty well in new surroundings. However, if the mother, by her character structure is used to getting her own way, or even to orchestrate the daily activities of her family, she will soon be in conflict with a stubborn child. Worse still, she will notice to her chagrin that the child, and not she, is the center of attention. Nothing worse can happen to an hysteric. And this happened to Anna when she brought home four-year old Joseph and was not prepared for his negative reactions. We talk about the time between the burning incident and his homecoming, and she is learning a lot from it. One might think that it is useless to talk about a time that will not return, but this is not so because it is quite possible that the time will recur in another form. Others may think it useful to talk about this period only to explain to the mother how she was "bound" to act the way she did. My purpose is not to explain past disasters but prevent future ones.

Anna had no problem with the second child that had remained with her since birth. After the burning incident with Joseph, the baby had been taken to his grandparents, and they still take care of it to enable Anna to work full time and help pay attorney fees. At present there is a gradual estrangement between Anna and her second child, and the possibility of similar difficulties when Anna takes back the younger child. In addition there is a small chance that Joseph, too, will be allowed to come back to Anna and his step-father. Then history may repeat itself, and the missing rapport between mother and child will disturb his upbringing and family life in general. It is of utmost importance that Anna become aware of the human interactions beforehand and can adjust her behavior so she won't panic in future crises.

"Preventing instead of explaining" means "working toward" instead of "working through." I am almost allergic to the term "working through" so popular in current psychology. A girl is overweight and is taken into play therapy to work through her complexes instead of working on a diet plan. A boy is a bed-wetter and is given non-directive therapy and allowed to throw wet sand at a wall to work through his guilt feelings instead of using the proven Enurex method. Another boy loses his father in a car accident and is taken into art therapy to work through his trauma, where he is encouraged to draw father figures and symbols, instead of exposing him to new experiences so he can slowly come to terms with the accident.

In working through, people reactivate, express, and discuss unpleasant events instead of working toward meaningful solutions by developing healthy attitudes or behavior patterns. I have found it more productive to develop something new instead of ruminating on what is past and cannot be changed. It is true that the new can develop from the old, positive from negative. The new may give meaning retroactively to the old that brought unhappiness but, seen as seed for something new, points to a positive outcome. One might say, "The justification for working through the old lies *only* in the development of something new which retroactively gives meaning to the old."

This is what Anna now realizes: all the insight she now has in her relationship to her children (which she and I discussed thoroughly) is the result of the catastrophe (which led to our discussions). She now can see that a child that cries, is stubborn, defiant, or destructive is not so out of wickedness but because it has not yet learned to properly relate to others. She also realizes that scolding and spanking will not improve the child's behavior because it only serves as a model for unhealthy behavior, making it more difficult for the child to learn to communicate positively.

Such a chaotic situation demands calm, patience, friendliness and firmness. Mother's firmness helps the disturbed child to orient itself, to gradually imitate her calm and friendliness. The health of the child depends on the health of the mother.

If treatment is to restore Anna's health, I have to start with her "hysteric character." Lecturing is of little use if she is unable to control her emotions. The main task is to teach her to give up instant gratification, acting on impulse, always playing a role, wanting to be the center of attention, blackmailing others with fainting spells or tears, to give up schemes of vengeance or attempts to force love by egoistic means.

After this glance into the abyss of trying to explain difficulties by tracing their causes, let's take a look into the other abyss—the mechanistic reprogramming of behavior patterns.

Some therapists would correct Anna's behavior by rewards and punishments. They would plan with her husband to deal out pleasant and unpleasant "reactions" to her behavior: not to talk to her for a day after an emotional explosion, or praise if a day went by without hysterical display. Or paste a gold star on a sheet of paper for good behavior and trade in ten stars for an evening out.

Such methods fade quickly as the novelty wears off. "Prescribed" praise seems artificial, the tenth evening out is less of a thrill than the first or second. One can always think of new rewards but this only fortifies one of the unhealthy characteristics of hysterics: their calculating nature. Soon such patients ask: "what do I get if I behave normally?" Normalcy becomes a matter of bargaining rather than a matter of course.

I have tried behaviorist programs with children but there always remains an aftertaste of the artificial. A girl was allowed to paste a have-a-nice-day face on a calendar for every day she didn't hit her little brother. She liked the game and the hitting was greatly reduced. But poor brother got more than his share on days when she hit him once "by mistake." She knew she couldn't expect any more "faces" that day and caught up with all she missed on previous days. Was this a successful change of behavior?

A boy received a quarter every day he did his homework. He saved to buy a radio and all went well. But one day his grandma sent him a twenty-dollar bill. He no longer did homework because he had enough money to buy his radio. The scheme was changed: if he did his homework he was allowed to listen to his radio. No homework, no radio. This worked for a while until he got tired of the radio and wanted to read comic books. Change again, but the mother said no: her son had to learn to take on responsibility without being bribed to do it.

Another boy was allowed to go swimming on Saturday if he did not take money from his mother's purse, as he often did. One day he took a twenty-dollar bill to buy a quartz watch. He said the watch was more important to him than the swimming. He also expected rewards for everything he did around the house. When he was to take out the garbage he asked: "what do I get for it?" This kind of behavior control works but has limits, it becomes mechanical subhumanism—behavior manipulated without relation to a value structure.

We could have manipulated Anna's behavior by reward and punishment but this would have reinforced her calculating nature. She had to learn to "do without" not for a negligible reward but for the sake of a person or value.

One thing she obviously valued was the relationship to her husband. He had taken her and her illegitimate child, endured her hysterical scenes with the two children, and stood by her during her trial. He loves her, and she knows it. Now she was to make small sacrifices "for his sake." We began with something harmless which, however, she found difficult: saving money. Often her husband had given her money for a certain purpose, like buying a new dress. While window shopping she saw something she liked, for instance a pretty rug, which she wanted right away. So she spent the money that was meant for a needed dress as a down payment for a rug, and came home without the dress but with a large bill for a rug she didn't need. The result was a fight. The husband was disappointed in her, and she was dissatisfied because she didn't get a dress. It ended with a hysterical scene, with smashed plates and torn shirts. Her husband, on such occasions, put her to bed and fled to his work because he couldn't stand home.

Her basic philosophy had to change from "wanting to get" to "wanting to please." We discussed a plan, and she followed through. The next time she bought a dress she chose one costing less than what her husband had given her to spend, and put the difference in a box. She cut down on smoking and placed the money saved in the same box. I encouraged her and told her how proud she could be of her little "sacrifices" because they proved she was not the helpless victim of her weaknesses. By summer she had saved $120 and presented the money to her husband as a contribution to a vacation. He was pleasantly surprised, gave her a big hug and took her out for dinner. Anna was delighted. The husband acted, in fact, pretty much as he would have been advised to act in behavior therapy, but he did it spontaneously, which made praise authentic and free of manipulation.

After learning to do without certain material gratifications, Anna had a more difficult task. At night, following upon a day of irritation she produced "nightmares," screaming and tossing in bed so her husband took her into his arms and comforted her until she fell asleep. But he could not fall asleep after such nightly incidents, and went to work all worn out. She was vague about the contents of her dreams, spoke of scary episodes with her children, being chased by someone, falling down a staircase, and similar scenes.

This was a rich field for dream interpretations but I remained skeptical. The dreams seemed to be addressed to someone, namely to her husband whose peaceful sleep was interrupted in a most unpeaceful manner. I asked her if she also had these dreams when her husband occasionally was on a business trip. She was amazed that she had no nightmares when she slept alone. I suggested the following: whatever her dream, she should not waken her husband because he needed his sleep so he could do his job the next day. She countered that she did not wake him on purpose, did not even know that she called out to him or moaned, and therefore could not control herself. I insisted she should try and make up her mind before falling asleep not to wake him up, come what may. This meant she had to "do without" any comforting embraces, and to do it for his sake so he could sleep undisturbed.

The result was that the nightmares disappeared. No one is happier than the husband who sees his wife getting better, and gives her no fewer embraces, not to calm down her hysterical outbursts but happy in a marriage no longer so stressful.

This procedure shows that the most obvious plan—disregarding the hysterical acts—would not necessarily be the best. If the husband had been advised to ignore Anna's nightmares, even if she screamed and groaned all night, the nightmares—in the long run—may have vanished. But in the meantime it would have meant tortured nights for both, with Anna producing more and more hysterical outbursts in order to force a reaction from her partner. He may not have been able to stand it and moved out or become violent, making the situation worse. Anna's voluntary sacrifice, on the other hand, made "staged" scenes superfluous.

Having proved to herself that she *could* be thrifty and *could* let her husband sleep, she had one more hurdle. Her tendency to lie, to be calculating and egotistical was to be countered by an antidote stronger than this "hysterical triad."

I thought I spotted the antidote: Anna's love for Joseph in spite of everything.

Once Anna tried to blackmail me to allow her to visit her son that day. But the guardian was out of town and without his permission I could not approve the visit. Anna promptly fainted.

I knew her character well enough and had also observed her jerky deep breathing (hyper-ventilation) by which hysterics often can produce short fainting spells. I placed an ice cold and dripping washcloth on her forehead, and this purposely clumsy first-aid succeeded quickly. When the cold water ran down her back, she abruptly woke and removed the washcloth. I asked her calmly to sit down and tell me why the fainting spell was necessary.

"It's about Joseph," she said, appealing to my pity, "I haven't seen him for ages...."

"What you did just now takes you farther away from him rather than bringing you closer. You showed the same behavior pattern as before, and uncontrolled emotional reaction. You can't throw hot irons at me, so you want to frighten me and show me what I have done. This behavior renders all of Joseph's suffering meaningless. Only when you change because you realize what harm your temper can do, only then will the child's pain and the humiliating court trial not have been in vain. Only then can our difficult work together lead to something good. Whether you see Joseph today or in a week makes no difference to him. But whether you change, whether you mature from guilt or pile on more guilt, makes a tremendous difference for Joseph. All you can do for him is to work on yourself, untiringly, so you do not repeat the horror you committed because now you are a different person." She understood: If she remained the same, her guilt and the child's meaningless suffering remained, too. If she changed, she could atone for the guilt on a higher level, and Joseph's suffering would become meaningful retroactively.

The idea challenged her tremendously, and it opened the possibility of a rehabilitation. She decided to work on herself "for Joseph's sake," as she herself put it. "For Joseph's sake" became our therapeutic argument for all further efforts. She had given up Joseph to others, taken him back, mistreated and hurt him—now her love would heal her and him. No punishments for Anna could protect Joseph as much as her guilty conscience, no award motivate her more than voluntary sacrifice toward character change. When she gets angry and is tempted to smash a vase, she stops—for Joseph's sake. When at work she feels that the boss favors a colleague, she "does without" a big scene—for Joseph's sake. When she has her period, she no longer uses it, as formerly, to play sick for a week, but pulls herself together and goes to work—for Joseph's sake.

This is what we have achieved so far, a continuous struggle because changes come slowly, every day relapses, but every day a slow movement forward.

Maturing takes its time and is based on the little phrase "for the sake of..." To do something for the sake of someone else brings warmth to even that coldest heart and bridges wide differences. In marriage counseling parents often remark disparagingly that it makes no sense to stay together "only for the sake of the children." Those who talk that way think of themselves, not of their children. It certainly is not ideal to keep a marriage alive for only *one* reason, but to do it for the sake of the children is a weighty argument. Parents, like it or not, bear responsibility for their children, and this has to be weighed against the often self-centered motives for divorce. Parents who stay together "only for the sake of the children" need to delete the deprecatory word "only" and rediscover a basis for their lives together.

Similar considerations are true for Anna. What she does for Joseph is not done "only" for his sake. It is connected with her own maturation toward responsibility.

Pessimists may say that this "repressing of emotional needs" will dam up Anna's feeling, that one day may burst and harm the child for whose sake she made so many sacrifices. We'll see if this theory holds, but we know one thing: The dam broke and harmed the child when Anna gave full vent to her emotional needs, on momentary impulse. By choosing to hold back, not repressing, our patient prevents a bursting of the dam. If she continues her actions for Joseph's sake, out of love for him, this could lead to a self-fulfilling prophecy, to the loving relationship between mother and son which had been in abeyance so long.

For some time psychology disregarded the possibility that we can find strength for the sake of an idea, a cause, or another person, without an ego-centered motivation. We are discovering that self-transcending motivation, reaching beyond our ego to the world outside, is stronger than animalistic drives because this expresses our own human freedom to act. If we want to tone down ego-centered motivations, we must encourage self-transcending motivations because egoism and self-transcendence are the two poles in our evolution between animal and angel. So far, we are closer to the "egocentricity" of animals than to the self-transcendence of angels.

To sum up:

Status at the Beginning of the Therapy

Anna's thoughts and actions center on the self ("egoism").

First step:

She learns to think about the problems of others. (Discussions of difficulties children have when coming back to the family after a long absence, considerations of solutions).

Second step:

She learns to think and act in a way that includes consideration of others (saving money for the sake of her husband, decision not to wake him up), to see the advantages of such actions.

Third step (present situation):

She learns to consider others in her thinking and acting not only for advantages (positive feedback) but also for *their* sake (atonement of guilt by sacrifices, thus maturing).

Decrease of egoistic motivation

Increase of self-transcending motivation

Learning leads from egoism to self-transcendence, away from the most important characteristic of hysteria to the most important characteristic of human socialization. If we move in that direction for the next 2½ years, Anna will have atoned for her guilt, and have discovered meaning in that guilt.

I once had a patient with a similarly tragic history. She told me about it and closed with these words: "All I have become was possible because in my youth I became guilty of a terrible deed. The awareness of this guilt changed me for the better. I can never atone for my guilt but all the good I did later, came from this awareness."

If Anna some day can say something like that, my work with her will have results I am hoping for. This case is presented not as a success story but to indicate possible treatment of guilt. One might consider guilt as a chapter in our life worth writing if it leads to better chapters dictated by a "will to meaning."

CHAPTER FIVE

RESISTANCE IN SUFFERING

Clients' resistance to psychological help and therapeutic planning is a matter of record and often justified. It may be based on common sense, directed against questionable interpretations, or express helplessness or anxiety in the face of the unknown.

Patients' resistance may contain a positive force which, used correctly, can serve in the therapeutic process. In fact, the attitudes of logotherapists themselves are molded by a certain resistance: they know about the unhealthy determinants in the patients' lives, they know the causes of suffering, yet they dare resist, fight and, if need be, negate the suffering.

Logotherapy may even be called a form of "resistance movement"—resistance against a psychologism which traces all human utterances—regardless of how true or authentic—to unconscious, mostly pathological motives. This is one of the two dangers mentioned in Chapter 1—the misinterpretation of genuine human problems on the basis of psychologistic speculations. Frankl illustrates this in the case of an American diplomat, in analysis for five years. He wanted to give up his diplomatic career which his analyst interpreted as an "irreconcilable fight against his father image." After long resistance to this interpretation the patient went to Frankl who recognized the patient's genuine desire to change careers because work at the U.S. State Department conflicted with his values. Frankl encouraged the patient to find work where this conflict was not present, and mental stability was restored.

In addition to the danger of false interpretations, therapists must remain aware of their responsibility. Little is gained by convincing a grown man of his "irreconcilable hate" of his (perhaps still living) father; it may cause or deepen stresses and bad feelings within the family. Nor is it helpful to indicate to a mother that she unconsciously hates her child, originally unwanted, but now raised the best way she can; this provokes resistance in the mother, also in the logotherapist. These unproven assumptions do more harm than good.

The healthy resistance of patients against devaluation of genuine feelings or motivations is directed against the dehumanizing tendencies of some pyschological schools. The "rehumanization of therapy" through logotherapy is a healthy antidote.

Rehumanization implies resistance against reductionistic therapy practices. I could quote many of my patients who would make a good case for a more humane application of psychotherapy. Patients with incurable or hard-to-cure illnesses often are told that their suffering is caused by stubborn resistance against therapy; they are charged with being unteachable, obstinate, and untrustworthy.

Case No. 20

Mrs. X had gone through various therapies including half a year of a self-discovery group that must have been a psychological striptease. Originally she had suffered from occasional twitching around the mouth, light anxiety and inhibition, and a limp. After group therapy she could hardly walk because her movements had become uncontrollable, face muscles kept twitching and occasionally made it impossible to eat because grimacing caused bits of food to drop from her mouth. She was made to feel that her sickness was her own fault. Her inferiority feeling worsened, she suffered from nightmares, and saw the simplest and most natural events as "symptoms of unconscious abnormal drives" or lack of ego strength.

At the start I did not know what condition was responsible for the unnatural movements of her body, nor could I estimate how much of her illness was "neurotic," caused by heightened irritation and inner tension after therapy. I suspected that only a healthy resistance against the unhealthy approaches of the group experiences could help her forget what she had been told, and her natural self-confidence would come back. This is what I tried to rekindle: her resistance.

Fragments of the dialogue:

Mrs. X: Next Saturday my daughter will have her confirmation. We have invited a few guests and I am full of fear. What if food drops from my mouth and everybody looks at me? It's true, I'm no good.

E. L.: Mrs. X, to be afraid of guests in your condition is not a sickness, it's natural. Every person gets embarrassed in distressing situations. And it *is* distressing to grimace in front of other people, and have food drop from your mouth. That this embarrasses you is proof that in your psyche you are entirely healthy. What is unhealthy are your disturbed body movements; your reaction to sickness is normal. In fact, I admire your courage that you make these long trips to our office. People in the bus and on the street probably stare at you. That requires a lot of spunk.

Mrs. X: But in the therapy group they all told me to admit that I am weak, dependent, and tensed up, and that my embarrassment is a sign of sickness.

E. L.: And I tell you that you are a courageous woman. Let your common sense decide whom you want to believe. What is more likely? That someone with a twitching face and body wants to crawl in a hole, or that she goes to parties, goes on shopping sprees, and mingles cheerfully with people?

Mrs. X: I think she'd rather hide.

E. L.: I think so, too. But you find the strength to keep house, come to me, go shopping, and even invite guests to celebrate your daughter's confirmation. Not many people would be able to do that. You can be proud of yourself.

Mrs. X: If you put it that way...maybe you're right. Maybe I'm not such a weak person...?

This example shows that resistance of a patient against unsuccessful therapy is helpful. As Mrs. X began to resist the thought pattern she had come to accept, her natural self-confidence returned. She gradually learned to distinguish her healthy from her sick self, and saw that only portions of her psychophysicum were affected, while in her human dimension she was still able to think and change her attitude.

Sometimes patients, after intense group experience, are so caught up in self-pity that they lose their independent thinking. For these cases I have developed a version of Socratic dialogue which I call "naive question-asking." (See case No. 21 in my book *Meaningful Living*). The therapist, by asking "naive" questions, leads patients to see their attitudes as unhealthy or even dangerous. This is done by the therapist seemingly accepting the unhealthy attitude of the patient. When the patients then continue their pattern of resistance, they resist their own unfortunate attitudes. This seeming acceptance of unwanted attitudes must be measured carefully, or the opposite- -a reinforcement of the unhealthy attitude—may occur. The correct measure can best be achieved through naive counter questions. The patients become unsure. They do not understand why the therapist reacts so unexpectedly. Instead of contradictions, they receive irritating agreement. This uncertainty is necessary for patients to question and rethink their "stuck" attitude.

Fragment of dialogue:

Mrs. X: I also feel a lot of guilt about my daughter.

E. L.: What do you mean?

Mrs. X: For instance, she often has bronchitis because I always kept her warm when she was small.

E. L.: But Mrs. X. that is no reason for guilt!

Mrs. X: (resistance based on fixated, unhealthy attitude): Oh yes, it's my fault, the girl is not used to cold and get sick easily. I've never been a good mother...

By means of naive questioning the attempt is made to redirect her resistance to the therapist to resistance against her baseless feeling of guilt.

E. L.: You always dressed your daughter warmly in winter?

Mrs. X: Yes, I did.

E. L.: (naive) So you wanted her to get bronchitis?

Mrs. X: No, no. I didn't want that!

E. L.: (naive) You didn't want her to become sick? What *did* you want?

Mrs. X: I wanted her to be healthy, that's why I dressed her warmly.

E. L.: (naive) Suppose you had been careless in dressing your daughter, without shawl and cap in winter, and with sandals and no socks in February. And later she came down with bronchitis because she had that predisposition. Then you would probably never have given it a thought that it might be your fault.

Mrs. X: I don't know. Perhaps I also would have felt guilty because I *didn't* dress her warmly enough. Yes, I think...without shawl and cap, I would have blamed myself.

E. L.: (naive) Then it's your fault in any case?

Mrs. X: Well, you never know what's best, do you?

E. L.: (naive) But if you do what you think best, you still have to blame yourself?

Mrs. X: No. If a person does her best she cannot blame herself.

E. L.: (normal) Right, Mrs. X, our fault is measured by intentions. You actually are to blame for all the sicknesses you *wished* on your child.

Mrs. X: (laughing) Then my fault isn't very great. I never wished sickness on anybody.

E. L.: Then we agree that the bronchitis can't be blamed on you but on fate as sicknesses usually are?

Mrs. X: Yes, that's true. That makes me feel better...

Logotherapy sees the human being as multidimensional, and the highest dimension, the spirit, is specifically human and thus relatively independent from others, the physical and psychological-sociological. Within the dimension of the spirit exists the possibility of a *healthy* attitude toward sickness in body or psyche, and this can help to stop the sickness, or at least make it bearable.

If there is an unhealthy symptom in the psyche (sadness, dejection, anxiety), patients, in the dimension of spirit, may gain a healthy attitude toward the disorder (accept sadness, find positive aspects to counter dejection, develop irony to thwart anxiety). They can take a stand against their emotional disorders. Frankl calls this opposition to biological, psychological, and sociological restrictions the "defiant power of the spirit." Neurotics are free to give in to their neurotic feelings or resist them. They can fear or minimize them, be slave or master.

To rally forces of resistance to a therapeutic process patients must use their capacity for self-distancing: the healthy spirit against the physical or psychic symptoms. As long as patients identify with illness, they are its victims, regardless whether they flee or fight. That's why the first step in logotherapy is often to arouse and strengthen in patients their capacity for self-distancing because this is the basis of a healthy resistance in a crisis: self-distancing means, among other things, to smile at oneself.

Fragment of the dialogue:

E.L.:   I'd like to ask you to do a little exercise, in connection with your eating problems. You are afraid the food will drop from your mouth because your face twitches.

Mrs. X: Yes, I think about it, and right away it happens.

E. L.:   Right. Fear makes come true what we fear. How would it be if we play a trick on the fear? When you do the exercise, disregard the fear. In the afternoon when you are home alone, sit down at the table with a sandwich, and make up your mind to eat it not once but four times. What I mean is: take a bite in your mouth, let it drop out, put it in again, let it drop out, and so on, until you get bored and swallow it.

Mrs. X: You mean, I should on purpose...?

E. L.:   Yes, for a change do the opposite to what you usually do. You don't wish to eat normally but want to find out how a sandwich tastes when it is eaten several times over. Okay?

Two weeks later Mrs. X reported that, to her surprise, she had less difficulties swallowing when eating her sandwich. She followed my instructions to drop the bites but it was easy to swallow them even when her face twitched around the mouth. She wondered how this was possible.

In fact, it is the effect of paradoxical intention that blocks the anxiety which causes the symptoms, and thus reduces them. Paradoxical intention is a form of resistance: the resistance of the patients to their own fears. To overcome resistance requires a tremendous effort, especially to succeed in normal life situations, like for Mrs. X to go to a restaurant with the firm intent to drop every bite at least four times in front of other customers. Yet, this technique—provided the difficulties are phobic—is the best method to conquer fear. We cannot fear what we wish for, and what we don't fear does not start any anxiety—thus the neurotic circle is broken. Humor is an essential aid in paradoxical intention because it is easier to intend to do something silly or exaggerated than to earnestly face the feared situation. Humor is a specifically human quality and, in the dimension of the spirit, remains free even in a crisis. Nothing provides more distance from our fears, weaknesses, and feelings of failure than a smile—it is direct expression of the human capacity for self-distancing, the most important help in actively resisting psychic disorders.

In the first phase of our dialogues, Mrs. X had been encouraged to resist her unhealthy interpretations. Now she learned to resist her anxieties. The neurotic overlay of her illness was reduced, and what remained was the organic part of her sickness: a choreatic syndrome responsible for the uncontrollable twitching. After having received her medical records I know that her spasms could be controlled neither by medication or psychotherapy. Brain surgery was not recommended because of high risk. Mrs. X faced the demand to bear this burden of unavoidable suffering. This diagnosis, however, became her rehabilitation because it proved that she was not an hysteric or obsessive compulsive case who needed to uncover repressed drives. Her organic sickness was bad enough. To further burden her with a psychic disorder would only drive her deeply into despair.

Our Socratic dialogues helped her distinguish physiological from psychological problems. By helping with the latter her suffering was reduced to the absolutely necessary minimum. All possibilities of active resistance (against false interpretations by others, against her own weaknesses and anxieties) had been exhausted. What remained was the difficult task of passive resistance against an unavoidable fate that threatened to destroy her psychologically.

The most important potential for passive resistance against any inadequacies, according to Frankl, lies in the human capacity of self-transcendence. It enables us to reach out beyond ourselves toward something important enough to dwarf weaknesses and symptoms and they cease being burdens.

Psychic distress that is no burden is no distress, and illness that is not taken too seriously, is no longer neurotically overrated. We often see that what counts is not what happens to us but how much it burdens. Self-transcendence eases the burden by focusing our attention and energy on something outside us, and our problems lose significance. Many examples show what people are capable of if they devote themselves to an idea, a cause, or another person; then their own problems fade away.

Frankl repeatedly stresses that we are not beings who just exist, but that we exist *for* someone or something with meaning for us. It is a great comfort for suffering people to realize that meaning does not depend on physical, material, or psychological wellbeing. Our affluent society proves that luxuries and comfort do not guarantee psychic health. The contrary seems true: a meaningful life in poverty is often a stronger basis for inner contentment than an empty life of meaningless wealth.

A psychology that sees us as being in pursuit of meaning must grapple with what is "the" meaning of life. Logotherapy has proposed a "Copernican switch" by suggesting that it is not we who ask life questions about meaning but life that asks us questions and we have to respond, be response-able. We answer life's question about meaning by living responsibly.

Fragment of the dialogue:

Mrs. X: My life is wasted anyway. Whatever I do, it's too late to change. And look at my trouble. I can't get rid of my spasms, there is no meaning any more.

E. L.:   I don't agree with you, Mrs. X.

Mrs. X: I know you mean well and want to raise my hopes that I'll get well again, but there's no chance.

E. L.:   I didn't say you'll get well. I said I don't agree with you that there's no meaning any more. Do you really think the lives of all sick people are meaningless?

Mrs. X: Sick people are unhappy.

E. L.:   Don't you think that healthy people are unhappy too?

Mrs. X: Yes, but...

E. L.:   You see, there are sick people who lead a happy and meaningful life, and there are healthy people who waste their lives without any meaning and are unhappy. I know sick people who have a severe illness and yet there is a glow of inner happiness about them. You'd be amazed.

Mrs. X: I believe you but for me this isn't possible. Perhaps they had a different kind of childhood, maybe their mothers showed them more affection.

This relapse into the negative interpretations of her group experiences had to be stopped by modulation leading to a positive attitude.

E. L.:   What counts is not only love we receive but love we give. You add both together and the sun brightens your life. If you received only little love you can compensate that by the love you give.

Mrs. X: (thoughtfully) The love you give...(pause) but if you didn't get enough love you can't give any, you are bitter, full of hate...

E. L.: Bitterness can be overcome if you have the will. You are not a machine, Mrs. X, that spits out what was fed in. Hate from hate, love from love—no, that's too simple. Of course, you cannot choose the direction you were steered by childhood, illness and personal suffering, but you have a powerful say in what you make of it all. Make use of it, have a say about your present life!

Mrs. X: What can I say to suffering?

E. L.: Every suffering has meaning if you only discover what it is. Without your illness, Mrs. X, you would not be sitting here and think about the meaning of your life. You'd probably be busy washing dishes, checking your children's homework, and all the daily chores. But perhaps it is important for you to think about your life, perhaps you'll discover something you would otherwise have missed.

Mrs. X: I have to think about what you said about compensating love you missed by love you give.

E. L.: Yes.

Mrs. X: It's true, a sick person can give love.

E. L.: Certainly.

Mrs. X: Then I could...despite my illness...I mean I'm not quite that useless?

E. L.: Mrs. X, this is your start to have a say about shaping your life! If you want to give love, you have plenty of opportunities, love is needed all around us. Think where are you needed, what task has been waiting for someone like you.

Mrs. X: I'll think about it. There's something I did before I became ill...I don't do it any more but I could start again. I collected used clothes and toys and sent them to orphanages in South America. If you knew how grateful these people over there are for any help! Yes, I'll start this again, I know the organizations, their

addresses, my illness will not prevent me. You are so
right, how could I have lost all my courage!

E. L.:   I can understand very well that you lost your courage,
Mrs. X, but you found it again in spite of everything,
and that is admirable. I consider you a very courageous
woman!

Logotherapy is education to responsibility through awareness
of tasks, values, and goals, and so enables patients to find their
own answers to questions of meaning. People have a natural
inclination to respond to challenges to become at least
coresponsible for their lives, rather than appearing helpless
products of their genes, past external circumstances, drives,
illness, and fate.

Realization that they are coresponsible for their lives leads to
awareness that they are free to shape their lives. This changes
resistance to hope, and self-pity to renewed will to live. If we
feel responsible for ourselves, we can't give up on ourselves, if
we see ourselves as cocreators of our fate, we cannot be defeated
by it. "People have freedom in any situation," says Frankl, "but
they often relinquish it. They can and must be made aware of it
again. Patients often say, 'That's the way I am,' and they mean
'therefore I cannot change.' In reality, they can change, they are
not static."

The collision of two hypotheses, "I can't change," and "I
always can change" often leads to struggle between logotherapist and patient, but as soon as patients see the basis of their
freedom no one can take it from them, even if illness severely
restricts it.

Mrs. X, too, found through work for South American
orphanages ways to discover meaning in spite of limitations.
This enabled her, by dereflection, to remove her ego from the
center of her thoughts and to develop a passive resistance to
brooding about problems. Her capacity for self-transcendence
and reconciliation with fate was demonstrated when her illness
progressed and she became bedridden in a hospital, seemingly
having lost all "freedom." "I spend much time praying for
people who are dear to me," she told me when I visited her, and
seemed quite serene. "I'll also pray for you," she added, "you
need much strength for your work." Her thoughts were not
dominated and darkened by suffering. She was guided by what
she still could do for others, and was tranquil.

Mrs. X is a living example that suffering has unconditional meaning. Through illness she matured to an extent which probably would have been beyond her as a healthy person. Spiritual maturity or physical health—who can say which is higher?

I have rarely conducted therapy where resistance played such a large role. First I had to rouse her resistance against what she had learned about a reductionistic picture of human nature. Then I had to overcome her resistance against my challenge to responsibility. Yet, this struggle led to a common solution: a health-bringing defiance to what could be changed, and a positive acceptance of what could not be changed.

Logotherapy teaches patients to revolt and find reconciliation by setting the powers of the human spirit against the powers of fate.

CHAPTER SIX

THE WILL TO JOY
AS HEALTH RESOURCE

Research in psychosomatic medicine shows the close interrelat-
onships between body and psyche: The immunity of the body
depends on emotional conditions, and vice versa.

This does not mean that we automatically become depressed
when ill, or that we develop physical illness after psychic shock.
Predamage (weak areas) in the body, which under normal
circumstances causes no trouble may, under psychic stress, flare
into physical illness; and predamage in the psyche may under
physical strain, trigger depression.

After an unfortunate event an entire family may sicken, each
member in a different area. Suppose father has a slight
predamage in his circulatory system, mother tends to irritation
in her digestive tract, grandmother has a pulmonary weakness,
but their immune systems keep them in check. One day the
family suffers from a traumatic event: the daughter elopes with
an undesirable partner. Weeks later father suffers a breakdown
in his circulatory system, mother develops painful gastritis, and
grandmother is taken to the hospital with pneumonia.

One cannot say that stressful events cause circulatory
trouble, stomach ulcers, or bronchitis. But they reduce body
immunity and cause illness where predisposition exists, however
unnoticed. One may compare this with a roof tile with a hairline
crack. It serves its purpose as long as the weather is good but in
a storm it breaks. The storm is not the cause but triggers the
break; if storms were the cause all tiles would break.

Predamage may also be present in the psyche: inborn
emotional tendencies are classified as sanguine, melancholic,
choleric, phlegmatic. Although we must be extremely careful in
typifying people, tendencies do exist, and vary in individuals. In

borderline cases between normal and sick there may be latent "psychological predamage" which surfaces when triggered by physical events. People who quickly become anxious, angry, or sad react emotionally if they are physically not up to par or illness influences their moods.

Figure 13. Psychosomatic Interactions

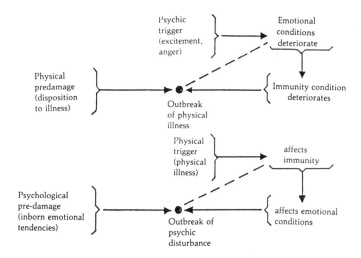

Figure 13 shows the significance of interactions between emotional conditions and immunity. The only factor under control is our emotional condition. We can do nothing about predamages, or psychological or physical triggers.

Our emotional condition is influenced by many factors, and one of them is will. If we can prevent major deterioration of emotion under stress, we may inhibit illness through keeping our immunity high. Frankl maintains that psychosomatic medicine can explain not only "why someone gets sick" but also "why someone stays well." We can stay well by using our will-ing power to stabilize our emotional state and thus increase immunity. As Frankl points out, if stress can be *triggered* in the psyche, it can also be *prevented* by the psyche.

We hear of people who fervently want to reach a goal although sick or dying. Their will to live and reach their goal strengthens their emotional condition and thus immunity. They live "beyond their biological means." "Overdrawing their health account" is possible only if urged by a strong self-transcending force: For instance a writer who wants to finish an important work (as Goethe his *"Faust"*) or a sickly mother to live long enough to see her children grown and independent. Such persons develop strength they would never attain if concerned mainly with their own interests.

Psychosomatic research shows how deeply psychological moods influence the body and also how physical conditions can be positively affected through awareness and active willing: We can stabilize our emotions through focusing on positive aspects of the world around us.

This is the opposite of unhealthy hyperreflection on ourselves and our situation, creating anxiety and doubt, weakening our emotional condition, and thus our immunity. The more positive aspects we notice in the world around us, the more positive our emotions (joy), and the more strength our organism retains for staying healthy.

Figure 14. How Dereflection Groups Work

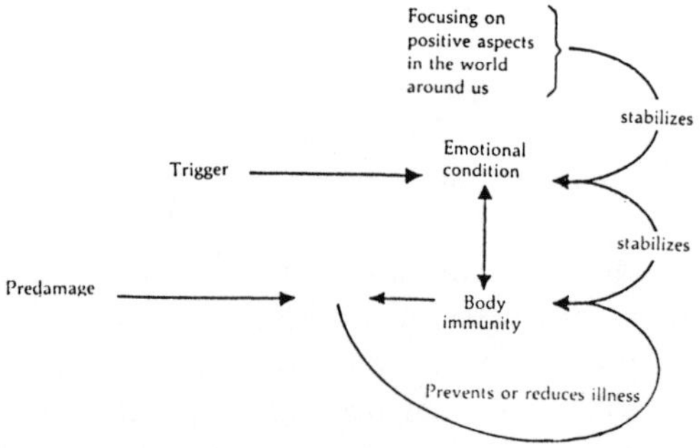

I developed a group therapy based on the findings of psychosomatic medicine, as illustrated in Figure 14. Though a trigger has adversely affected emotional condition, and predamage exists in the physical organism, focussing on positive aspects in the world around stabilizes emotions and immunity, and thus prevents or reduces illness.

In most other group therapies participants talk about personal problems. This may worsen their emotional condition and increase hyperreflection. Consequently immunity will decline, increasing chances for physical or psychological illness. However, groups have certain advantages:

1. Participants learn that other people have similar problems.
2. By discussing their problems in front of others they become less inhibited.
3. They hear other ideas about how to solve their problems.

I have tried to retain these advantages without the disadvantage of hyperreflection on problems (thus possibly weakening emotional conditions and immunity). Because we focus on positive aspects in the world around us I call these groups "dereflection groups."

Case No. 21

Here is a summary of the first dereflection group conducted several years ago. Subsequent groups showed similar reactions.

At the first meeting of the group I stated the ground rules in approximately these words:

We have met here because we all have a burden which we have carried and hope to relieve in these sessions. This is a special group, a "dereflection group." In other groups, participants share their troubles and look for ways to overcome them. In our group we will focus on our strengths and capacities. Instead of fighting what is ill and weak, we will promote what is well and strong in us. Either approach can overcome suffering.

To achieve our goal I have to limit your "freedom of speech" a little. You may talk about whatever you wish except your unsolved problems and the depressing descriptions of your illness.

Not that I don't want to hear about your problems or that I expect you to "repress" them. I only ask you to consider the other participants who find it difficult to focus on positive aspects in their lives if constantly confronted by the negative. If you have a problem, please talk to me and we'll make an appointment. Topics for group discussion are ideas, suggestions, and reports that mirror joy—something pleasant you have experienced or thought about.

Perhaps some of you think that you don't have much cause for joy, but every day has positive moments. We have to notice them, and sharpen our ability to do so.

The positive moments need not be conspicuous: a potted plant where buds are opening, a meeting that warms the heart, a photo that brings a beautiful memory; a weakness overcome. You may talk about problems if you tell us how you solved them; we learn from that and gain pleasure from it. "The world is not perfect but perfectable," Frankl has said. This is to be our guiding sentence in this group: "My private world is also not perfect, but perhaps it too is perfectable."

The first reaction was spontaneous agreement among the participants. They liked the idea but it was difficult to find positive things to share. They had no experience in expressing joy. It was easy to talk about problems. These were at the center of their attention. But to share joyful events? The ensuing silence was a symptom of a "joyless" society which had forgotten how to take note of the positive.

I used the silence to present a poem, and have found it useful, at similar moments, to have suitable poetry ready. At that first dereflection group I read a poem by Phil Bosmans:

Strange, incomprehensible life.
Year for year, day for day
You move among people and objects.
Some days the sun shines,
and you don't know why.
You are happy.
Strange, incomprehensible life.
Year by year, day by day
You move among people and objects.
Some days the sun shines,
and you don't know why.
And you are happy.
You see the beautiful side of life.
You laugh, you are grateful.
You want to leap for joy.
Work is easy.
Everybody is friendly. You don't know why.
Perhaps you slept well.
Perhaps you found a friend
and feel yourself understood, safe.

You think: That's how it should be —
peaceful, profoundly peaceful.

Then, suddenly, everything is different.
As if the bright sun brought clouds —
Sadness befalls you, inexplicably.
All seems dark.
You think no one likes you.
In trifles you seek reasons
to complain, to grumble, to envy, to accuse.
You think that's the way it will be forever,
Nothing will change,
And you don't know why.
Perhaps you are tired. You don't know.

Why does it have to be that way?
Because we are a part of "nature,"
with days of spring and days of autumn,
with summer warmth
and winter cold.
Because we follow the rhythm of the sea:
Ebb and flow.
Because our existence is a constant repeating
or "life" and "death."

If you understand this, you can go on
with courage and faith, because you know:
After every night comes a new morning.
If you accept this,
These ups and downs,
it will help you gain greater depth
and joy.

Some participants were touched. They could identify their
mood changes with images in the poem. After the session, at
home, they looked for similar positive meditative material from
books and magazines. They realized how much support can
come from a good book or a good thought, that this can be a
wholesome nutrient in a crisis. But all this was still imitation.

Then one participant had a creative idea. He knew that
positive contributions in the group were expected but could not
remember anything positive lately. He therefore started a "diary
of beautiful hours." Every evening he wrote down what

beautiful things the day had brought. This forced him to look for things beautiful and, according to the proverb, "He who seeks shall find," he did find suitable incidents. He observed children helping an old woman cross the street, and felt good about it. He received massages and felt relaxed afterwards. He took a walk through the woods, enjoyed the fresh green. Never before, he said, had be been aware of the singing of birds. Since then he opened the windows in the morning to listen to birds and found it easier to face the day.

He confessed that he had never expected to find so much material for his diary. Other participants took up the suggestion and decided in various ways to sharpen their sense for the positive. Two, independent of each other, tried an unwritten diary of beautiful hours. In the evening, before falling asleep, they let the events of the day pass in review, picking out the positive. Both reported that they fell asleep faster, slept better, and dreamed positive dreams.

Here, for the first time, the therapeutic effect of dereflection was demonstrated and became applicable to the group. Many suffered from sleeplessness and mentioned the curious fact that they often fell asleep during interesting TV shows but tossed and turned in bed when they wanted to sleep. They now found the explanation: shifting attention from concentrating on sleep to other, possibly positive contents of thought. Sleeplessness in the group improved without further discussion.

Occasionally I had to help the group over low periods, by readings or guided fantasies. Associations of ocean tides and mood changes helped them back to positive aspects. Without knowing anything about paradoxical intention, some particip-ants discovered paradoxical behavior as a way to overcome bad moods, and even with humor.

One woman reserved jobs she liked for "low days" when she felt despondent. Such jobs brightened the day. Another added the idea of making use of days when she felt energetic, by tackling strenuous jobs she had postponed. She saved the needlework she loved to do for days she felt low, and major strenuous house cleaning for times when she felt hyperactive. Others decided to try this idea.

Next session there was much laughter. They had waited for especially hyperactive or depressed days but none came. Moods remained stable; the disturbing ups and downs, because paradoxically intended, flattened out.

Gradually my part in the group became minor, limited to gentle steering. I had to intervene once when one participant talked about failing as a commercial artist. He accused himself of allowing others to use him and thus heading into frustration and resignation. His presentation became more and more negative, his body language expressed an unhealthy self-pity. The other participants listened gloomily.

I stopped him and gave him a "special task." He had broken the original agreement, other group members also pointed this out to him. As "reparation" he should make a special contribution to the group. He should make up a list of possibilities how his artistic talent could be used. He was to prove to the group that the negative can be made a positive, weakness to strength, if there is the will to do it. I was prepared to have an individual session with the man if he could not find a healthier attitude but I need not have worried. He reported to the group that he had gone through his many sketches and drafts and come to the conclusion that it was a waste of his artistic talents not to make good use of them. He had decided, despite all discouragement, to make renewed efforts to get suitable commissions, and had ideas. For instance, he intended to work on restorations of folk art and to contact the National Heritage Foundation which sometimes needs volunteer experts. Museums, too, need people to restore paintings and antique furniture. He had many interests and was confident he would at least find occasional work, and this would satisfy him.

By re-valuing himself, he transcended himself. He paid attention to the world outside. The diary of beautiful hours and the paradoxical treatment of moods were still ego-centered ideas. The intended use of talents included consideration of creative values—going beyond the self since creativity requires material that has to be worked on and changed.

We know from behavior research that change in itself significantly influences our lives. Behavioral scientists who often work with animals conducted the following experiment:

1. They gave caged chickens the chance to get a food pellet by pressing a button, which the chickens quickly learned.

2. They then gave chickens the chance, by pressing a button, to ring a bell or change the light in the cage. The chickens learned equally quickly to press the button and did it with the same eagerness as in the food experiment.

Since chickens have no biological or any other gain from ringing bells or changing lights, it was concluded that the *change in itself* brought "psychological gain." The wish for change, observable even in animal psychology, is another refutation of the homeostasis principle which underlines the innate wish for unchanged equilibrium.

Conclusions from animals to humans are to be taken with caution but the same correlation between conduct and change has been discovered by humans, especially in drug addiction.

For some time it was assumed that addicts use drugs primarily to brighten moods, overcome inhibitions, sadness and anxieties, and raise the level of living. But some addicts use drugs to attain the opposite—to calm down, relax, fall asleep. The desire for a quick change in activity level, regardless in what direction, is now considered a decisive component in addiction. Here we see also the link with the motivational theory which maintains that lack of meaning creates a climate favoring addiction. Logotherapy agrees with experienced physicians that "nothing is more deadly for the human brain than when nothing happens."

If we assume that humans (and even higher animals), in addition to other needs, strongly desire occasional change, we still must ask *what* has to be changed. For the chickens it was the outside world, for addicts it is the world within. Normal, healthy people in contrast, seem to be primarily looking for changes in the world, for living rich in variety—vacation trips, theaters, celebrations, outings, hobbies, visits of guests, etc. We may suspect that the psychologically sick are fixated on changes within while healthy people enjoy creating changes within and outside.

This working hypothesis is supported by two observations confirmed by therapists:

1. For most patients changes within seem more important than those in the world outside.
2. As patients become healthy, interest in outside events is rekindled.

Dereflection works this hypothesis backward: it tries to rekindle interest in the outside world to help patients regain health.

Our discussion about art objects opened a door for group participants that had been closed for some time: the door to the outside world.

The group began to talk about paintings, beautiful old buildings, jewelry, and all sorts of collections. This led to lively discussions about such worldly topics as shopping, possessions, and investments. Good and not-so-good things were mentioned and I noticed that they dwelt more on the good things without overlooking the not-so-good. Until recently any minor negative event was enough to wipe out all positive aspects of their lives. Some began to see the whole picture and accepted the negative without surrendering to it. One woman who had several collections, raised the question of their meaning because the pieces "only gathered dust in a closet." At this moment she considered others because collections have meaning only when people see them. The woman and other group members discussed what kind of people would enjoy seeing their collections, and one man decided to contact a friend to swap stamps.

The outside world of things, and now also of people, was rediscovered, and the "thou" became increasingly prominent in our discussions. The diaries of beautiful hours more and more often mentioned friends and relatives contacted by mail and telephone.

One participant made a film of a trip and showed it at his home to the group members and other guests. Another participant was interested in homeopathy, and brought books and art articles to help group members. Since his advice was appreciated he broadened this to help others among his acquaintances. A woman brought a picture book, *Jonanthan Seagull*, and explained its symbolic significance. As a consequence, others in the group bought copies to give to family members including young people.

Through attention to interpersonal relationships our discussions became richer; there was hardly enough time during our group session to discuss all the contributions. Their projects filled evenings and weekends; instead of complaining about empty, sad evenings they now complained of lack of time.

Group members hardly noticed inner changes because they didn't observe themselves and their problems but talked about interests in the outer world. When I expressed my delight about the change, they pointed out that this was the first time they were asked to direct attention to positive aspects. Where in the world, they said, do you see something positive? The news media are full of catastrophes, dangers, and problems. I told them that this was true but that our ability to discover positive aspects did not depend on the impact of outside influences. The positive is within us. We cannot force it on anybody, nor can we recover it from someone who has it.

There are many kinds of joy, most induced not by our will but by our emotions, wellbeing, or gratification of needs. The joy we found in our group was a special sort, consciously discovered, originating in the will. "Some scientists will deny the existence of such joy," I told the group, "but you proved them wrong. You were weighted down by worries, you went through difficult times, your psychic condition was not the best, but you had the will to joy, to see the positive, and that was enough. Nothing, whatever the situation, can deprive you of your power of willing, not even severe suffering. It can influence your emotions, your wellbeing, your needs gratification. It can make your material possessions seem irrelevant. But no one can take away your positive experiences if you don't want this to happen. Even during an incurable illness the positive in your life remains yours, a sacrosanct memory. Nothing can wipe out the events you recorded in your diary of beautiful hours. What you wrote down is part of your life forever. It is the true harvest of your life."

At the last group session I told them an Indian legend to emphasize the importance of dereflection: One day a dog wandered into a house of mirrors. Wherever he looked he saw himself—a dog. The many dogs irritated him, he bared his teeth and growled. As he noticed that all other dogs, before, behind, and next to him also bared their teeth, he became scared. He barked at the nearest dog, and in his excitement did not notice that the barking, resounding from all sides, was all his own. He only saw angry faces, bristling hair, and started to run. First slowly, but the other dogs ran too, so he ran faster and faster, and the others kept on his heels. He couldn't get rid of them. Terrified, he tried to flee from the other panting dogs, hours in circles until he collapsed dead, chased by no one but his own image.

The group participants understood the warnings: persons who see only themselves are similarly caught. They volunteered to say that their group experience would keep them from being lured into the house of mirrors of egocentricity, from shutting out the world and getting into a disastrous self-isolation.

The balance sheet of the dereflection group showed that many psychological symptoms receded though some remained. Participants had become a group of joyful persons with problems that seemed lighter. No iatrogenic damage was done, and beyond that a number of positive results:

- Despite my offer, only one participant asked for an appointment to discuss personal problems.
- Upon my question at the last meeting the participants confirmed that they had not missed not talking about their problems.
- My participation was reduced as individuals contributed more and more positive experiences by themselves. This was proof that they were increasingly aware of positive aspects in their lives.
- Although few participants noticed changes within, almost all were able to enrich their outer conditions with meaning.
- The group experience itself was enjoyed by all.
- During the ensuing months no one developed serious illness except that one man had a slight accident.

One, or even a few group experiments with similar results, do not prove our working hypothesis that the dereflection group procedure stabilizes the emotional condition and improves the immunity of the participants. But nothing occurred to disprove the hypothesis.

Frankl's concept of the human being as a three-dimensional unity implies that joy, and emotion, do not belong exclusively to the dimension of the psyche. Joy is also part of the spirit and affects the organism. Whatever influences us affects all three human dimensions.

I know of a pastor who participated in a group therapy because of his attacks of migraine. His attacks occurred regularly after meetings with church elders. It was assumed that the migraine was caused by stress, and the pastor was to "work through" his anger and anxiety in the "safe atmosphere" of the group.

The group sessions, however, created doubts in the pastor who became unsure after having been forced to reflect about himself and his conflicts. He was encouraged to reveal the inhibitions he suffered in the company of others, and the secret frustrations and aggressions he was trying to hide. He came to believe that he really suffered from inhibitions and defense mechanisms which made it impossible to function as a pastor. He found it difficult to give his sermons which had never been any trouble. He resigned and withdrew to a religious retreat.

But his migraine became more frequent and he went to a doctor who discovered that the patient had an allergy to a certain kind of floor wax. It turned out that this floor wax was used in the room where he met his church elders and also in the dining room of the retreat.

This case history shows how every psychotherapeutic treatment affects the totality of the patient. At the start, the migraine was merely a matter affecting the body; in the end, body, psyche, and spirit played their part.

It cannot be stated that in a dereflection group the migraines would have decreased (though we don't know what part the immune system plays in allergies). But it is clear that in a dereflection group we would also have discussed the positive experiences in the pastor's meetings with the church elders. He would have realized that his migraines could not have been caused by anxieties, inhibitions, and aggressions because these also came after very positive meetings. Perhaps this would have led him to consult a physician sooner instead of getting psychological (but not the best possible) help.

I have argued that dereflection groups eliminate much of the risk of other group therapies. Does such a dereflection group at the same time retain the three advantages of group therapy listed in the literature?

As mentioned, the first advantage is that participants learn that other people have similar problems.

Participants in a dereflection group learn that others can master problems, that they can laugh in spite of problems, that even in dark hours there are glimpses of joy. This, I believe, is at least as great an advantage.

The second advantage concerns the need to speak about one's problems in front of others, and thus become less inhibited.

Participants in a dereflection group are encouraged to talk about positive things in front of others, and thus look for and find positive aspects in their lives. That their inhibitions are reduced comes as a by-product, a significant one.

Advantage number three deals with the possibility that they can learn from others how to solve their problems.

The dereflection group deals with the possible expansion of

healthy and "problem-free" areas. That some problems were solved was again pure side effect. No solutions were offered. Group members found them by themselves and became models for one another. This may be the greatest advantage of the dereflection group.

Early in this book I mentioned that the history of psychotherapy starts on a negative note: attention on what was sick and abnormal and had to be uncovered. The next step was to pay attention to positive and negative "stimuli and reactions," both of equal importance.

Today we have reached a new stage. The dereflection group is proof that psychotherapy has found a therapy form that emphasizes the positive.

CHAPTER SEVEN

PSYCHOTHERAPY
AND RESPONSIBILITY

About ten years ago, psychologists discovered the phenomenon of dyslexia. A few children had trouble in spelling and required special treatment. This had no relation to intelligence. To avoid frustration these children were not graded in spelling during remedial work. A good concept, and yet...

I witnessed the beginnings of the dyslexia boom in the psychological counseling center. We were confronted with increasing numbers of dyslexics who, while treated, were not graded in spelling. But the number of dyslexic cases grew faster than could be treated. Teachers received special training but soon did not know what students *not* to include in special classes.

Eventually the extra load was too great for the schools and the concept of dyslexia was eliminated: No special grading, no special classes, no special therapy.

Our counseling center continued treating children with spelling difficulties and we experienced a surprise. Within weeks almost all dyslexic children changed back to normal. Since schools no longer offered special treatment, the interest of parents and teachers in this particular therapy declined. Even stranger, misspellings also declined; the children—with few exceptions—were no longer "dyslexic." Meanwhile a new method to accurately diagnose dyslexia appeared.

I mention this unintentional "experiment" because it illustrates "responsibility in psychotherapy." It shows that psychotherapy can not only cure but create disorders. There is good reason to suspect the behavioral problems of many children, and symptoms of psychologically unstable adults, exist because they were diagnosed as such!

One rarely hears of clients being refused treatment because they don't need it. Yet, people seek psychological help for all kinds of reasons: they feel insecure in their own behavior, in relation to partner or children, and often through reading of psychological or self-help literature. To regain courage and self-confidence, people need encouragement and help. Treatment may do harm when focused on what they conceive as "illness."

The best therapy often lies in guiding clients to their healthy inner resources. The real question is what responsibility lies with the therapist and what remains with the client. Certainly childhood traumas and faulty learning processes may influence behavior but we must be careful not to make them into alibis. A recent TV program announced:

"Uli is an unruly boy, he defies his parents, does as he pleases, plays hookey and refuses to study. Who have failed—parents or school?"

Television bombards us with such deterministic assumptions--someone is guilty but not the person himself—"poor Uli" is not responsible for being rude and lazy.

Court testimony by psychologists occasionally goes in this direction. Here is an expert opinion quoted in the case of a motorcycle thief:

"The key to understanding the present personality must be sought in the psychological damage done to the accused within his first two years. The traumatic event, although forgotten, remains alive, and potentially dangerous, it threatens and fills with fear the conscious part of this person through the influx of dark archaic impulses in his present life . . ."

The trauma which is discussed here to explain the theft of a motorcycle turned out to be the "disturbance of an infantile oral phase": The accused, in his early infancy, was taken off breast-feeding and put on the bottle.

If I may be allowed a personal reference: My own early days were characterized by nightly air attacks which necessitated my mother's waking me from deep sleep and hiding in a cold air raid shelter, in constant fear that our home would collapse or go up in flames. This trauma should be enough to excuse my stealing a long column of huge trucks.

Frankl repeatedly stresses the danger of presenting human beings as mere victims of circumstances. It is part of the essence of our humanness to feel guilty, just as it is part of our humanness to accept and possibly redeem guilt. "Take guilt away from a person, and you take away his dignity," are wise words, not very popular today.

Young people in particular are quick to find "excuses" in psychology, and this blinds them to their real chance and challenges. Focussing on the "pleasure principle" makes them overlook the "power of will."

Case No. 22

(Part of a dialogue with a student)

She: I go through such depressions, I can't enjoy life.
I: Do you have reasons for depressions?
She: My grades were poor.
I: Can you improve them?
She: Yes, I'd have to study harder.
I: Why don't you?
She: I don't feel like it.
I: Who or what is at fault for your unhappiness?
She: The poor grades.
I: No.
She: That I don't study enough?
I: No.
She: That I don't feel like studying?
I: Not that either.
She: What then?
I: That you make the amount of study, which you yourself consider meaningful and necessary, dependent on your moods.

It *is* possible to study, even if one doesn't feel like it, if the goal is worthwhile. Logotherapy maintains that in our noetic, our specifically human dimension, we *can* stand against our drives, impulses and moods if we consider the goals important. The "will to meaning" (Frankl) dominates over the 'will to pleasure" (Freud) and over the "will to power" (Adler) because we are primarily meaning-oriented. We are not helpless victims of "complexes" and "animalistic demands" but are able to take responsibility for ourselves and the world around us.

Of course, we must not misconstrue as "excuses" those inner and outer factors which do influence psychological moods or illnesses. Logotherapy acknowledges their importance, but qualified—not every deviation has a psychological cause, at least not in the present state of our science.

Psychiatrists are expected to find fitting explanations for every murderer and terrorist. All sorts of hypotheses exist that use repressed emotions and dammed up hatred to justify episodes of killing of innocent people. Such hypotheses must be viewed with caution. Is an unconscious hatred of a mother really sufficient excuse for a brutal rape? Does an inferiority complex really explain assaults and robbery of elderly people? Would it not be more honest to admit that we can find no, or only vague explanations for certain human behavior, especially abnormal behavior? I am convinced that criminal excesses are not caused by "too much" (emotional disturbances, complexes) but rather by "too little" (compassion, responsibility, self-discipline, social understanding). Is the decisive factor for a cruel act of aggression really hate and anger, or simply indifference?

Not every human action can be completely explained, at least not until the human brain develops to a higher level. We cannot explain everything retroactively, nor does a "psychological cause" necessarily lead to particular behaviors. There are stressful circumstances that do not lead to abnormal excesses. If psychological consequences were not anticipated, people would often be spared suffering.

A woman asked me: "I recently went through a divorce, but I feel okay. Tell me, why don't I have the divorce shock we read so much about?" A man who worked intensively in his profession wanted to know why he had not developed a manager sickness, why his stress did not cause illness. These two, anxiously observing themselves, *can* develop their shock and illness. Similarly, the "midlife crisis" often occurs by worrying in advance about it. Logotherapy, emphasizing the power of will, started a counter movement against a tragic determinism. It stresses the responsibility of the individual for his or her actions. I have seen how emotionally damaged persons, in a Socratic dialogue, regained awareness of responsibleness and changed almost overnight. Instead of focusing on what could not be changed, they learned through dialogue of areas where they could control their actions.

Case No. 23

How largely dialogue controls psychotherapy, is illustrated by the following case. The "dialogue" was mainly "logotherapy by correspondence." The client was a young man who needed help but because he lived at a distance could seldom come in person.

His problems became evident through the letters he agreed to let me publish. The interchange illustrates the importance of underlining the positive, leading the client to greater independence and responsibility.

June 5, 1979, from Mr. X's letter to me:

I told you on the phone that I was able to overcome my compulsive obsession by paradoxical intention on my own. I greatly appreciated you congratulating me on my achievement:... As I gather from your reply you place much stock in "achievement." I believe we expect too much of children in school. Only the most intelligent succeed. All my life my relatives pounded into me how important achievement was. I was forced into professions which did not correspond with my true talents. To please my family I worked like crazy in jobs I detested. Result: Nervous breakdowns, circulatory problems, heart trouble, and finally intensive care in the hospital... This question bothers me: is the existential vacuum a neurosis in a clinical sense? I would appreciate your clearing this up...

June 11, from my letter to Mr. X:

That you escaped your compulsion on your own is indeed a great achievement, and this is also what I meant by "achievement"—a growing beyond yourself, an action or attitude which can make you proud. It does make a difference whether one is pressured from the outside—"overdemanded"—or overcomes one's own weaknesses by the "defiant power of the spirit."

You write that you performed work at detested jobs for the sake of your family. Perhaps this was needed during that phase of your life—to find out what you really wanted and could do. Perhaps this suffering helped you mature, so you could know what really is meaningful to you. To blame others helps little in finding one's own way.

The existential vacuum is no neurosis but fertile ground for neurosis to develop. But I would suggest you not worry about existential vacuums or neuroses but actively start shaping your life according to your potentials and desires. Perhaps a step-by-step approach will help, a listing of all those actions that can bring your goals closer. Don't take too big a step at once, enjoy every little success! Regain your trust in life, the rest comes by itself.

June 20, from Mr. X's letter:

Thank you for recognizing my "achievement" in freeing myself from a severe 17-year obsession. Compulsive brooding made me unable to work. Since I was 15 I read much on psychology, psychiatry, and philosophy. Then came a period of questioning—I wrote about 300 letters to authors and universities. I was searching for truth, meanings, and values. The answers from the professors didn't satisfy, they contradicted each other. My brooding worsened. I had conflicts.

Two years ago I discovered logotherapy, and salvation. However, in frequent fainting spells after a myocardial attack, a psychiatrist thought my condition was caused by the psychological cure through paradoxical intention. Paradoxical intention as the cause of illness? I could not believe it. An internist had a different opinion. He explained my troubles (cold, sweaty hands and feet, blood congestion in the head) as after-effects of the myocarditis. I had many illnesses during childhood and youth. I feel that psychiatrists think every person who resists psychiatry needs treatment. They can diagnose any behavior as abnormal or sick. Once a psychiatrist poked his finger toward my eyes. When I drew back, he said, "You are neurotic." This really happened and I could cite more examples.

I am enclosing a book on psychology. Please tell me what you think of it . . . If I were an expert I'd have my own opinion, but I feel helpless against authority. They decide about our lives, what is normal and abnormal.

July 7, from my letter to Mr. X:

First, I sympathize with your difficult situation and appreciate your interest in expert opinions. But don't overestimate the opinions of experts (whatever their field). Psychotherapists are more competent if they have lived through their own crises and emerged healthy. Others theorize about conditions they have not experienced. The book, of course, is depressing and I read it with mixed feelings, but I don't take the aberrations of psychology tragically because eventually they are revealed as aberrations. Nature's process of selection also goes for psychotherapy—only those methods survive that contain timeless truths.

As to your own situation, don't be tortured by doubt about what is normal or abnormal, what others think of you, and what is correct. We all have a voice within that tells us what is correct. You may call it "conscience" or something else. This voice is a good guide.

July 20, from Mr. X's letter:

On leaving the hospital my writing is still a bit shaky, but I want to write this letter to show I can do it.

My heartfelt thanks for helping me in this difficult time through your letters and phone calls. No one else sympathized with my difficult situation.

I am home again, and I have been told that I'll have pain for a long time to come.

Allow me to relate more about my obsessive compulsion. Last night I awoke with strong palpitations. I had an obsessive dream—the whole city was full of bookstores, and these full of thick, scientific books. They scared me terribly. Actually I have not been in a bookstore for months. I had to take valium but when I awoke the next morning the anxiety was gone, thank goodness. How do you see the interpretation?

July 24, from my letter to Mr. X:

A quick reply before I go on vacation.

As to "obsessive-compulsive dreams", to "mystify" dreams can be dangerous. You can laugh about dreams, and the more scary they are the more you can be glad they are "only" dreams. Of course in times of crisis our dreams often are scary or confusing which proves that our minds are active even when we sleep. During crises the mind must be more active because it has to work on overcoming the crises. Writers, artists and inventors in their creative stages have periods when they sleep badly and dream a lot, because their minds cannot switch so quickly from creativity to "pause." That's why dreams can be a useful gauge of mental activity. It all depends on interpretation. Imaginative as you are and with a tendency to reflect, you are likely to have many ideas about your future—unless you get stuck on past and present problems.

Let your imagination guide you, and you'll discover possibilities you can at least partially realize. Make use of the positive in you, do not brood on the negative!

You were told you will have pain, but you were not told that you'll also feel joy. You have no control over pain, but you do have control over joy! Let the joy win out—you are brave, you can succeed!

Sept. 3, from Mr. X's letter:

In our personal conversation I have learned that sexual behavior, too, can be determined by our conscience. I am now free of guilt feelings, you know what I mean. (See Case No. 1).

There is a particular question I had no time to ask when I saw you. How can one protect oneself from the consequences of stress relief after overcoming difficulty? There are no general rules, are there?

September 16, from my letter to Mr. X:

As to possible consequences of stress relief after overcoming a difficulty I can only say: If we like to have problems we will always look for them, even when some are overcome. What is difficult or not, stressful or not, we determine ourselves, and we also determine whether we are happy having overcome the difficulty, or brood about the consequences of stress relief, thus creating new difficulties.

Indeed there are genuine problems and objective suffering, but many people create their own suffering, without wanting to or even knowing it. That's why I suggest that you think about problems that are real and need to be solved. All that superfluous brooding, fearing, and doubting wastes valuable time in which you could do something positive or experience something beautiful if you keep your mind open for the unused possibilities around you.

I know you go through periods of illness and unemployment and may have to face many a dark hour. But don't lose confidence that this too will have necessary and meaningful consequences. You have gained insights during this period of suffering and are able to mobilize your strength for a meaningful future.

Oct. 23, from Mr. X's letter:

Many thanks for your letter which contained so much spiritual nourishment. This one today is to prove that your words have landed on fertile ground. You made me realize that we do not need to know "everything" at any price. Too often the price for my wanting to know was part of my health. You wrote quite correctly: All this superfluous brooding only wastes valuable time—I have often experienced that! Now I have dropped my brooding, it has become clear that it is wrong to live according to "psychological textbooks."

December 5, from Mr. X's letter:

The year 1979 nearing its end was one of maturing for me. The blows of fate had meaning. I don't think it is helpful to ask myself at every decision if it is the correct one. That's what I have a conscience for—to make responsible decisions.

I have a few questions left. Frankl writes: Whoever stands still will be overtaken, and whoever is self-satisfied loses himself. How exactly are these words to be understood? I think there comes a moment when we must realize that we have reached our limit... Although I have been without work for a long time, I have developed no unemployment neurosis or frustration. Am I justified saying this, based on my feelings? Can I recognize what is sick and healthy?... Some authors recommend reading to keep mentally healthy. What are the chances for simple, uneducated persons? Not everyone likes to read. How much free time should we fill with such centripetal activities?

December 13, from my letter to Mr. X:

Try to be yourself. If you were what you ought to be according to the books, you would not be yourself! Don't look for unemployment neurosis if you don't have one, and don't worry whether your free time is filled by centripetal or centrifugal activities, as long as you know what you like to do. And don't observe your weight—you are neither too thin nor too heavy. Certainly, reading keeps you mentally healthy, but whoever dislikes reading will find something else. Where is the problem? My dear Mr. X, we all face the task of reducing our problems rather than enlarging them. We try to solve little problems as they crop up, before they choke us in their totality. Perhaps this is what Frankl means with "not standing still"—not stopping the work on ourselves and the world around us, to regain the good, beautiful, and the healthy, often denied by nihilistic thoughts including those in books you love to read. I personally do not believe that we can ever reach our limit because the human spirit is able to expand even in old age, as many people have shown. The only limits for the spirit are the obstacles we ourselves put up. Many examples testify that our inner strength cannot be broken even in hopeless situations if *we* do not give up. On the other hand, some people in the most fortunate circumstances yield to a despair they have talked themselves into... Take courage, forget brooding over psychological textbooks, and don't build obstacles to that freedom of your spirit. I am convinced that many tasks await you that no one else can fulfill.

March 27, 1980, from Mr. X's letter:

I'm sorry my latest visit took up so much of your time, and I sincerely thank you for your extraordinary patience. Forgive me for "bothering" you again but I still have a few problems which I can see now because obsessions no longer cloud my mind, and because I have thought a little about my past.

My family always teased me about my constitution. Father forced me to eat, mother touched my hips and said, "look how your bones stick out!" In my youth they always told me to study, study, study. Mother helped me with homework... She hit me with her fists when I didn't understand something. I developed a fear of school, hated the phrases my parents used to quote such as "Knowledge is Might."

In contrast to father, mother wasn't educated but was a valuable person though addicted to alcohol. My grandfather always said, "as the twig is bent..." Please comment.

I am happy to be mentally and psychologically well again. Physically, too, I have improved. I hardly gain weight, but health is more important than weight, isn't it? Only now that I have overcome my neurosis can I live according to the Indian saying: Act so during the day that your dreams are tranquil at night."

April 10, from my letter to Mr. X:

It seems almost that you treat me like an oracle who always decrees the truth. You really don't need this any more. It may reassure you to hear my opinion about various subjects but you are well equipped to form your own opinion and that alone has validity. Your childhood memories have many negative undertones, is this really necessary? It certainly is possible that there were negative factors: your frequent illnesses, contradictory and partly strict upbringing, downgrading, school anxieties, etc. As you know, much depends on attitude; there must have been positive things too. You were nursed back to health, criticism of your bony hips showed that your parents worried about you. Similarly I suspect that your mother's wish for good work in school was motivated by hope that you would get a good start in life.

You see, parents do make mistakes, and children do have shortcomings, but everyone can mature through weaknesses, during parenthood or in mastering one's own life.

I know the saying "as the twig is bent" and of course we all have hereditary traits but we have the responsibility about what we make of our inherited traits—whether the twig will bear fruit or become barren... I am glad that you found a new job, and that you made up your mind not to give up easily. These are steps in a healthy direction leading away from brooding. Don't forget, the value of every undertaking is in proportion to the effort put into it—the harder it is to stick to it the greater your "achievement" and the prouder you can be of your ability to see it through.

June 27, from Mr. X's letter:

Meanwhile I got away from self-observation and attended to the tasks life—or I myself—put before me. I do exercise without watching myself in the mirror all the time. It's all right to look in the mirror, but with the correct attitude! It is important to me now to see confirmed what I always suspected—that I'm a psychopath. According to a book by Dr. M, a psychiatrist, a psychopath is someone who is unable to adjust to social rules and requirements, and suffers from this inability. The genetic code of the psychopath is faultily programmed, he says. I don't belong to the aggressive but to the sensitive type who suffer from uncertainty. Dr. M also sees Jesus, Buddha, Marx, etc. as psychopaths.

Now you'll ask why I am again into psychiatric literature. In my present state of mind books no longer harm me.

July 3, from my letter to Mr. X:

I must commend you: you hardly ask questions any more, which proves you no longer are uncertain, and you find your answers, have your own opinions and express them. Good for you.

The book by Dr. M you might as well have skipped. You are no more a psychopath than Jesus or Buddha. Apparently you don't know "real psychopaths." I do. They are people whose conscience does not "function" and who therefore brutally hurt the feelings of others, torment them sadistically, and for their own advantage trample over others. There are no "sensitive psychopaths," believe me, because it is this very lack of sensitivity toward others that characterizes them. Just erase the word "psychopath" from your vocabulary and be glad you have not encountered a "real" one.

July 7, from Mr. X's letter:

I recently read that the will can never be the motivation for action. Formerly such views would have disturbed me, plunged me into brooding. Today I can read such thoughts with almost frightening unconcern. I am a happy person and feel fulfilled.

What I wrote today I did without compulsion, no obsession drove me to it as it did last year.

August 18, from Mr. X's letter:

It's been a while since I wrote to you, and I consider it a good sign that you didn't answer my last letter immediately. We don't want to get stuck in a "patient-therapist dependency." A little child will run to mother with every little problem, but it's no good if this goes on after the child is grown up. At first I didn't accept my responsibility and came running to you like a little child and depended on your help. That's over. I applied at various companies and have been turned down without a reason given. I am used to this. Rejection is nothing new. I don't give up because I tell myself that by trying again and again I take responsibility into my own hands. I'm enjoying my kitten and am not ashamed that it enriches my life. As is my custom I bought a scientific book about cats.

Sept. 16, from my letter to Mr. X:

Am glad to hear you're well. That the kitten enriches your life I can well understand. To take care of an animal is a responsibility, and the more responsibility we take the more we grow in our tasks.

Sept. 23, from Mr. X's letter:

Your "suggestions," your comforting words, your explanation have helped me become "a new person." Of course, my life still has crises but I can handle them better. I am still concerned about my sense of uncertainty when exposed to scientific views, but they are a barrel without a bottom. I admit I feel best when I try to find my own answers to the questions of life, or—to quote Kierkegaard—to find a truth which is truth for me. In this connection I want to tell you that your letters were liberating... I am enclosing an article "The Beautiful and the Ugly"—unfortunately there are academicians who base their value judgments on appearances, and I feel accused by them.

October 6, from my letter to Mr. X:

As to the article you sent me, I cannot really see that it says "value judgments are made based on appearance." As I understand it, the author expresses the cliche that beauty and happiness are two different things, and the external appearance of a person brings advantages and disadvantages. And this is good because if a person's appearance would hold only advantages, there would be no challenge. So the mixture is ideal. As normal persons with "a little beauty" and "a little ugliness" we are motivated to make the best of ourselves, at the same time keeping out frustrations and stresses.

October 23, from Mr. X's letter:

> Your last letter was very instructive. I was angry about a sports physician who told me: "Well, you will never look like a Russian weight-lifter!" I am allergic to the words, "You'll never..." I really was upset and lost four pounds, became dizzy and had palpitations. But I have absorbed the words of the physician and regained the four pounds.

November 10, from Mr. X's letter:

> I greatly appreciate that at my last visit you devoted so much time to my problems... I am proud that I have overcome physical and physiological illnesses through changes in attitude, healthy nutrition and exercise, and have become a healthy person able to take action. As to exercise, I'd like to ask a final question: the sports physician probably cannot acknowledge my achievements because it has been scientifically proved that people with weak bodies have dark muscle fibers which do not respond to training, while athletes, with light muscle fibers, respond well. I ask myself: what motivates me to do the training? Probably an unconscious inferiority feeling... But I consider training and sports important because they hold experiential values for me—they make me feel better.

November 25, from my letter to Mr. X:

> You ask me a question but you know the answer. You are just a bit uncertain and want to know whether your answer is correct. Now, grow beyond your uncertainty and remember that your answer is right for you.
>
> It is possible that you initially were motivated to exercise by an unconscious feeling of inferiority. As a young man you obviously suffered from such feelings, and it is quite an achievement to have dealt with this suffering constructively—to become fit. Why then

devaluate this achievement by saying exercise is nothing but a compensation for inferiority feelings? Even if the original motivation was physical weakness, your achievement is the more admirable because it shows that you wanted to overcome your weakness.

I really don't think that your original motivation is still the same. When you write that sports for you is an experiential value, this no longer has anything to do with inferiority feelings. You probably have found pleasure in exercising, and that's why you are continuing. Pleasure is a motivation in itself, one need not look for hidden complexes. Forget about brooding over whether you have dark or light muscle fibers, and whether you'll ever look athletic. If you get pleasure from exercise, that is motivation enough—what else do you need? Have fun in your training!

December 28, from Mr. X's letter:

Many thanks for your kind and informative words. I took them to heart! Your main goal was to help me regain and build up self-confidence. You'll be pleased to know that you succeeded. A simple example: In your preceding letter you mentioned I should not brood over whether I'll ever look athletic. That hit home; I simply enjoyed the exercises and didn't expect results beyond that. And do you know, after a while I noticed new muscles. Indeed, self-forgetting and self-confidence are keys to success!

I have given away all books on psychiatry, psychology, and philosophy. I feel liberated, feeling entirely myself now. More than that: After a long struggle I have accepted personal responsibility. That's what I want to tell you—no questions, no doubts. I have a permanent job, and will make use of my musical talent—I'm going to take piano lessons!

Thanks for everything, best regards, and a fulfilling year!

After a paper I read at a medical meeting a colleague told me: "I don't think too much of logotherapy, but I'm sure that some of your patients give up their symptoms to please *you*." The man was not aware that he entirely agreed with the basic concept of logotherapy: that (neurotic) patients have the *freedom* to give up their symptoms for whatever reason.

Mr. X had the freedom to give up many of his, frequently severe, symptoms. That he made use of this freedom was not entirely "to please me." But if our correspondence, by using modulation of attitudes, dereflection, and development of a wider value orientation contributed to health, it fulfilled its purpose.*

The close link between psychotherapy and responsibility confirms the need for a psychotherapy that dares to include the resources of the human spirit. This does not mean we should exclude other methods. Logotherapy needs the entire scope of medical and psychological methods of other schools, but without logotherapy these other schools are insufficient in dealing with the increasing frustration of our contemporaries.

Logotherapy presents a return to values, meanings, and common sense—no new discoveries but the wisdom of the ages. Frankl reports that his first books published in the United States were welcomed as "finally something new." But on his lecture tours in Japan and India he was told: "These are the old truths of Shintoism and Buddhism but expressed in the language of modern science!"

Frankl combines new and old ideas about the nature of the human being that is helpful in curing and comforting. These ideas can be summarized in three words:

Challenge to Responsibility.

This challenge goes for patients *and* psychotherapists.

---

*When this book was published one year after his last letter, Mr. X had normalized his life, was successful in his work, and his private life was satisfactory. He had completely given up compulsive brooding.

CHAPTER EIGHT

Reflections

REALIZING ATTITUDINAL VALUES

When Frankl speaks of meaning fulfillment, he mentions three values—creative, experiential, and attitudinal. We find meaning by what we do, what we experience, and through the attitude taken in unchangeable situations. There is a paradox: He sometimes speaks of the three values as of equal rank, but sometimes he speaks of attitudinal values as the "ultimate" or "highest" way to find meaning.

This paradox puzzled me. For a long time I was inclined to consider creative and experiential values "higher" because they issue from free will while attitudinal values are forced on us by Fate. It is my choice to repair a broken machine thus realizing a creative value, or to enjoy sunset on a beach, realizing an experiential value. I could have chosen to do something else. I have no choice, however, if I am sick and helpless in a hospital. I *have* to bear my suffering, bravely or not, so I may as well make the best of a bad situation.

But I now know it is not that simple.

I learned this while finishing my studies at the bedside of my mother who was dying of cancer.

We desperately tried to find words of comfort during her last days, but she began to *comfort us* and developed incomprehensible strength although her body became weaker and weaker. She "realized attitudinal values," not to find meaning, and certainly not to make the best of her hopeless situation, but for *our* sake. She acted with courage, not to overcome her own suffering but to alleviate ours. It seemed impossible but she succeeded.

Her example gave us strength from which I still draw in hours of despair. When I tend to lose heart over a trifle or become anxious in a relatively harmless situation I remember her serene attitude and feel ashamed of my dejection, and am able to let it go.

Since then I know why Frankl ranks attitudinal values so high. When we realize attitudinal values we become an example, and this contains a hint of immortality. Every example is passed on to others; it has no meaning without relationship to others. An example transmits itself by motivating others to do likewise, and new examples are created for the next "other." This is true for positive as well as negative examples. Attitudinal values, if realized, are truly positive examples, the *propagation of the good*.

Compared to this, creative and experiential values pale in significance. They are primarily for our own gain, and only secondarily useful for others. I do not want to belittle creative and experiential values, especially in the form of love; they underpin our lives. But they are not free of egocentricity or clearly distinguishable from "lower" motivations of needs gratification. In creative and experiential values purpose and value overlap. The building of a one-family house satisfies the "nesting instinct," the need for security, perhaps for power and prestige, while at the same time fulfilling the meaning of a particular stage in life. Experiences are always closely linked with emotions and drive gratification. Their values lie in the "more" beyond the instinctual. For creative and experiential values it is difficult to estimate how much self-interest and need gratification is behind them, and whether they are to be interpreted through depth psychology or by a height psychology that includes explorations of spiritual longings as well as psychological drives.

Not so with attitudinal values. They cannot be explained by depth psychology. There is no gratification of needs, no gain, no self-centered purpose. It makes no difference whether a person dies courageously or complaining. Complaining may even be easier. If a man loses his sight and demands sympathy and help from others, he will probably gain more than if he realizes his attitudinal values and tries to face Fate on his own. What distinguishes attitudinal values is that they benefit others, and not necessarily the person creating the new attitude. Frankl says of persons realizing attitudinal values that "they bear witness to what a human being is capable of." By bearing witness these persons set examples of achievement that live on in their "audience."

In 1979 Professor Frankl himself demonstrated to he how he realized attitudinal values. He didn't discuss it, he *lived* it. During a visit in Munich he suffered a severe heart attack and was taken to an intensive care unit. The next day I reached his wife at the hospital and she handed the telephone receiver to her husband. He told me that his condition was serious and that his heart could stop beating any moment.

I wanted to say so much to help, comfort and thank him, but I couldn't find words. Here, like mother at her sick bed, was a person who had more strength than the people around him, and set an example. He spoke calmly, almost happily. To die held no terrors for him, he said, because he had just finished a task (delivered the manuscript of a book to his publishers). The responsibility had been taken from him, he need not do anything to change the situation, it would be decided for him. He accepted any decision of Fate because it was beyond his responsibility and therefore could not be wrong. He also expressed his pleasure in so much human kindness even when surrounded by cold, electronic hospital equipment: the friendliness of other patients, the efforts of the team of doctors, the presence of his wife. He had devoted his life to the rehumanization of psychotherapy and would not leave this earth without receiving human kindness up to the very end.

Thus, he tried to comfort me who myself could not find words. He wanted to tell me: "Remain calm, too, when you'll face death some day. Look, it's easy, you need not be afraid." This was his legacy, a lesson from the hospital bed. He did not think of heart failure—he thought of me!

Having witnessed this demonstration of attitudinal values, I know what is meant by the logotherapeutic concept of "transforming suffering into a human achievement." It always refers to an achievement attained for others.

Professor Frankl fortunately recovered but his example, which I hope to be able to pass along, will survive us. These incidents convinced me that attitudinal values may be considered "higher." They also made me understand the link with the other values. All three are equal in the sense that they make up the entire span of human meaning. There is no meaning fulfillment that does not manifest itself in at least one of the three values.

I discovered this when working on my dissertation. I asked 1,000 persons selected at random what they considered the most important meaning in their present lives. All answers, diverse as they were, could be classified, without exception, within one of the three values. In round figures, 50% were creative, 25% experiential, and 25% attitudinal. For this reason I speak of an "active" and a "contemplative" half of the human meaning horizon.

I did not immediately realize that here was the key to the paradox because I misunderstood the equal rank of the three values to be an either-or. In reality, it is not that we realize one value or another, but that *everything* we realize—all that is positive, good, and meaningful—belongs to the totality of the value triad. Equal rank does not mean the three exist next to each other, but that they make up a unity with differing emphases, with room for *every* meaningful human thought, act, striving, feeling, and suffering.

This helps me to make use of the logotherapeutic value system in counseling. I no longer think I must motivate clients to realize one of the three values—this only arouses resistance. I know now that everything positive in the clients' lives is reflected in the totality of the value triad; I need only to help them find the positive (as in the dereflection group), for them to realize their lives are filled with meaning. It is a mistake to believe that life is "empty" or "full of meaning" like a sack with few or many socks. Life has meaning under all circumstances even when unnoticed. We have to draw the attention of the suffering client to what is left instead of what is missing. There is a great deal left—in every situation.

From case histories we can see that Frankl works with "what is left." In his most quoted case he speaks of an old man in despair because he had lost his wife. Frankl asked him what would have happened if *he* would have died first. The patient answered that his wife would have suffered terribly. Frankl needed only to point out that the patient's wife was now spared this suffering, but at the price that the patient bear his. The patient's statement "I am suffering" was countered by Frankl's "You are suffering *for her*." These were the magic words that elucidated the attitudinal values against the background of the total value triad and gave the suffering man strength to bear his pain. Attitudinal values are unthinkable without an "other." The meanings they help us find depend on a "Thou," a "for Thee."

People facing unavoidable suffering must come sooner or later to attitudinal values. They are part of the myriad stars in our "meaning firmament." Because they function as example one might call attitudinal values "superhuman"—transcending the sphere of meaning of the suffering person.

Case No. 24

I once debated with an elderly and very intelligent man why he should bother to go on living. He was paralyzed and had no relatives. "My death will hardly be noticed," he said. The word "hardly" was the one that mattered. His suicide would be noticed, even though "only" by strangers. People would say, "Another poor fish ended his life because he could not stand it any longer." Young people would read it in the newspaper and, in a desperate situation, might also consider "ending it all."

The more people solve their problems in a particular way, the more do others follow. The more drug addicts, the more people will "also try." The more transsexuals reported, the more uncertain will others be about their sexuality. And the more people commit suicide, the more will others rashly throw away their lives.

"I know you will not commit suicide," I told the old man. "I know you have a strong sense of responsibility—not to a child or grandchild but to your fellow humans. Otherwise you would not have come to me for advice. You know, the negative, the weak, the evil, spreads easily and fast. People like you can help spread the positive. Others will take courage from your courage, to bear their suffering, They will find hope in your example when they need it."

The old man is still alive. I write his story to spread his example.

THE MEANING OF DEREFLECTION

In discussing the best possible help for suffering persons during the therapeutic phase, three logotherapeutic methods were mentioned: Paradoxical intention, dereflection, and modulation of attitudes. Of these, modulation of attitudes was discussed more fully because it affects the grimmest of suffering—the kind that cannot be avoided.

Of the other two, paradoxical intention is well covered in logotherapeutic literature, as more important than dereflection. But this is false because dereflection, as shown in previous chapters, is of great help for suffering persons.

Dereflection is based on the exclusively human capacity of self-transcendence, the capacity to reach out to others beyond our own needs and drives, to include others in our considerations.

Self-transcendence does not come easily. For this reason, dereflection is not easy to apply. But its application is vital. Dereflection is more than a psychotherapeutic method, certainly more than the diversionary maneuver for which it is often mistaken. It is not merely a move away from what is weak in us, but toward what is strong. It is a thrust into the dimension of the human spirit. Both dereflection and self-transcendence are massive counter measures against the frightening and psychohygienically unhealthy egocentricity which today seems on the increase.

The metaphor which clarifies dereflection for me is that of a lonely sailor in a small boat, riding the waves of the wide ocean, under the infinite firmament. Here you have the three dimensions of the human being: the sailor trapped in his boat as we in our body. It provides shelter but if it cracks the trip is over; neither ocean nor sky will come to his rescue. The wide ocean surrounding and carrying the sailor inextricably tie him to our planet, just as our psyche ties us to our body. The psyche reaches far beyond the body but both form an entity, like boat and ocean together making the sailing possible. The firmament above is like the "meaning horizon" of the human spirit. It is beyond our reach, yet always present. It is a dimension that rises above water and boat into the sphere in which only human beings can take part. Only the human animal can stand up on its hind legs and reach skyward.

But our sailor can see the firmament of the spirit only when he looks up. He must hold on to the mast of the boat tossed by the waves of his psyche. But even if he looks not up but horizontally across the ocean, he catches the reflection of the firmament in the waters—distorted but clear enough to assure him that the firmament above exists. The higher he stands the wider the area of reflection he can see. If he crouches down and looks just barely over the edge of the boat, his field of vision shrinks. This is also true of ourselves. The more distance we have from our psychological processes the wider is our overview. The "look upward" can be compared with our capacity for self-transcendence, the "look into the distance" with our capacity for self-distancing.

But what happens when our sailor crouches down until his forehead touches the floor of the boat, on all fours like an animal? Then he sees nothing but his immediate surroundings. Nothing exists for him but himself, his small pathetic self tied to the tiny nutshell of a boat. Here you have the egocentric human being.

Dereflection is liberation from egocentricity, from hyper-reflection on the self and its problems. Only lifting the sailor from crouching to an upright position will enable him to see the expansion of the firmament. A gentle lifting of the chin is rarely enough. Clients trapped in egocentricity, foreheads touching the floor of the boat, have to be lifted up, and that requires an immense therapeutic effort.

Sometimes I get the image of myself and clients, grappling with each other in the shaky boat, the patients crouching, I pulling them up. I try to get them to look above the edge of the boat, to loosen their grip, to enable them to see the wider picture and thus gain health.

Case No. 25

A young mother came to see me for half a year, always complaining about trivialities. A word from her husband upset her, a dream frightened her, a change in the weather made her irritable. Eventually I realized her real problem: the woman thought exclusively about herself. She was preoccupied with her health and, as a result, felt miserable.

I looked for the value horizon in her life and found to my amazement that she had four small children at home. Four children, and a mother who only thought of herself? At our next session I paid no attention to her complaints and began talking about the world of the child—how it develops, how it gains its first impressions of the world, the importance of the first childhood experiences.

The young mother showed little interest, but I continued in subsequent sessions to talk about the miracles of the growing human being. Her expressions of groundless self-pity became gradually less strident, perhaps she noticed that I did not respond to them.

Then, one day, she asked me a question which did not concern her own personal interests. She noticed, she said, that one of her boys was slow in developing his ability to talk. She even suspected a possible speech defect because he could not pronounce certain words.

Here it was, the first glance above the edge of the boat, the perception of something outside her self: A child whose development was in danger. "Now she must not fall back," I told myself. "I have to support her, hold her, capture that self-transcendence which we are so painfully reawakening."

It would have been easy to refer her to a speech therapist, but this was not my plan. The mother herself would have to take over the treatment of her child, not for the child's sake, but the mother's, by way of dereflection. I taught her exercises to help the child overcome his speech defect. The mother gradually developed a talent she had not suspected. She followed my instructions and read the pertinent literature, in an effort to bring the child back to normal. She became aware of the needs of her other children and made little check lists noting those needs. Her attention to the children had a feedback reaction from her family, in joy and gratitude, so that my role as counselor became increasingly superfluous. Today, the boy started kindergarten, free of speech defects, his mother satisfied with her place in life. A self-inflicted suffering had been relieved by dereflection.

Recently she visited me again and her first words were: "How are you, Frau Doktor?" On previous visits her first words usually had been "Oh, Frau Doktor, today I feel miserable!"

While paradoxical intention brings suffering to an end,

dereflection often requires suffering to set in motion the spiritual development of a person. Just as the mother outgrew her trivial problems because of the speech difficulties of her child, so in times of crises people are stimulated to achievements never dreamed of.

Dereflection is not so much an end as a beginning: the beginning of the evolution from "patient" to "human being."

Dereflection is a difficult therapeutic task. Birth is never easy, neither the birth of a body nor the birth of spirit.

THE QUESTION-ANSWER GAME OF FATE

Humans are the only earthly creatures who are future-oriented, who can plan ahead.

But life planning, as in chess, cannot be done too far ahead. The long-range goal is to win, but short-range goals must remain flexible, depending on the moves of our opponent.

Contrary to a chess partner, our opponent in life does not plan. Fate moves by chance, it plans neither for or against us. This indifference is harder to take and more frightening than a planning opponent whose moves we can perceive and counter. With Fate, we never know if it will help or harm; it lifts or crushes us without apparent reason.

In therapy, too, chance plays a part. Accidental events have often helped my patients regain health; in other cases they counteracted my best efforts. What could I do, for instance, when a middle-aged woman whom I had helped overcome a depression learned that she had to have a mastectomy because cancer was suspected? No wonder she suffered a relapse.

But chance also helped with my successes. I struggled in vain to help an elderly woman with a severe noogenic neurosis. Then, by chance, a refugee camp for Vietnamese refugees was set up in her neighborhood and she volunteered to help the children. While she was collecting toys, clothes, and blankets among her friends, spending hours mending and repairing, her neurosis disappeared. (This case is more fully discussed in *Meaningful Living*, pp. 104/5).

Chance is a powerful opponent. In our chess game with Fate we cannot win, but *how* we play the game determines how meaningful our life is.

Logotherapy helps people find meaning in an experience in which chance plays a decisive role. A mother who just buried her child asks why this had to happen. A woman raised in an orphanage wants to know what she had done to deserve this fate.

A planless universe offers no comfort. It is no help to believe that injustice happens by accident, that the child's death and being raised in the orphanage are meaningless acts of Fate.

We search for explanations but find only causes. The cause of the child's death was sickness, and the cause of the need to be brought up in the orphanage was the death of parents. This does not explain why these tragedies happened. "Fate does not plan," is the only answer we can give to these most searching questions—a depressing answer which logotherapy helps us transcend.

Logotherapy has no explanation for cruel acts of Fate, but it can help find a meaning potential behind a nonplanning Fate, and more: it can help find some ultimate wisdom behind the depressing chance quality of life.

The wisdom is that the meaning of Fate lies in our response to it. Apparent random events attain meaning through challenging our reactions and attitudes. Our silent opponent in the game of life is not an evil and overpowering foe who takes chessmen off the board against all rules of fairness. Its function is to keep the game going. Sometimes it forces us to move under duress, choosing among painful alternatives, occasionally we find ourselves threatened by a checkmate.

"It's not up to us to question but to respond," is the message of logotherapy, and herein lies the secret of good players: they don't waste time and energy questioning the opponent's move, but concentrate instead on the best countermove. Nowadays, chess players play against computers. Here the comparison with Fate is even more appropriate. The players are not interested in defeating a lifeless machine but in the game itself, to try their skill and respond to the challenges to the best of their ability. In the chess game of life we, too, don't know what Fate has programmed, yet we are obligated to match it move by move.

Good players concentrate on winning moves—in life, meaningful moves. They will respond to every move of Fate by taking responsibility for their own moves. Logotherapy stresses that we are responding to the challenges of life, that we are "response-able," able to respond to the meanings offered to us in every situation.

We live responsibly when we counter fate with human planning that is flexible, conscientious, and responsive. We are flexible by keeping our options open yet remaining true to basic values and goals. We are conscientious by listening to conscience when the next move is up to us, even when we move under duress. And we are responsive by responding to the moves of our silent opponent, by finding meaningful actions and attitudes to its moves regardless whether they fit in with our original plan.

One of my doctor friends, a religious man, has five children, the last-born a mongoloid. He was shocked to realize that all his medical knowledge was not sufficient to cure the child. But he found a meaningful response: "My wife and I try to imagine how God, as He deliberated to whom to send this handicapped child, decided on us as a family because He trusted in our strength to give this child as much love and protection as it needed. We are thankful for this trust and will try to show ourselves worthy of it."

He conquered the random accident that so pitilessly determined the chromosomes of his fifth child by a conscientious life plan which lovingly included the child. The parents might have angrily swept the pieces off the chessboard or resigned from the game. They might have kept asking agonizing questions as to why this happened to them and what had they done to deserve it. Instead of fighting and questioning, they responded. Their life plan had to be modified by the birth of the fifth child but Fate was not able to change their goal—to live a meaningful life.

The meaning of chance lies in our response. Only we can decide the meaning or meaninglessness of accidental events. Chance decides what happens, but we decide how to take it. Chance has power over our life, but we have power over its meaning. Perhaps we are not such unequal partners in this game after all.

MEANING versus GAIN

To go for gain beyond what we have is a universal human

ambition, and because logotherapy is concerned with the total person, logotherapists have to recognize this aspect of human nature too.

To *gain* is a source of joy; to *have* soon becomes saturation. Enjoyment is the result of previously having done without. The first warm ray of sunshine after a long winter brings more joy than hours of sunshine during summer. The first wobbly step after a long illness, the first bite of food after starvation, are great sources of joy. If gain follows gain, the contrast is lost, and the result often emptiness or addiction to abundance. Europeans who remember the war years of scarcity enjoy present affluence while the young generation suffer from existential vacuum.

Meaning is more easily found when affluence follows scarcity, not the other way around. Scarcity elucidates meaning because it motivates us to overcome it. It is a motor fueled by awareness of a purpose, a "what for." To bring an end to scarcity, to build a better life, are powerful goals. When these are attained and a period of plenty follows, the contrast to privations overcome makes the achievement a source of great joy.

But when the sequence is reversed, and you have known nothing but affluence, there is no exhilaration because you have not experienced the contrast. You are not motivated to change anything, the "what for?" has no answer. Why do anything if you have everything?

Scarcity after affluence is considered as terribly unfair, a reason for despair. A loss is not easily accepted. The spoiled child cries for its broken favorite toy, and the impoverished rich show similar withdrawal symptoms. Affluence taken for granted without joy is followed by scarcity taken as unbearable burden.

Affluence is a blind alley. But we cannot expect the prosperous to throw away riches. What we *can* do is to switch the sequence from joyless affluence leading to despair, to meaning fulfillment leading to joy. This we can do by applying the motivations that work during scarcity, even if the scarcity—as often happens—exists in the midst of plenty. We have to find a "what for." The "what for" in scarcity is obvious: to overcome scarcity. In affluence it is more difficult—to find something that motivates people to use their strength, inner resources, and "will to meaning" to reach a goal, change a negative attitude. Our clients must be shown how to switch joylessness within affluence to fulfillment within scarcity, regardless whether it is scarcity of outer or inner resources. The result is regained capacity to enjoy life.

Let us see how this approach worked in the cases mentioned. The young mother tied up in her trivial neurotic complaints had no material worries but felt empty and without joy. Her emptiness found content once she became aware of her son's speech defect. Suddenly a crisis required her help. She still lived in affluence, but now there was a challenge. She threw herself into the strenuous but fulfilling task to dedicate herself to the needs of her son, and subsequently of her other children. She was on her way to meaning.

Similarly, the elderly woman overcame her noogenic neurosis through a literal change of scenery—the establishment of the nearby refugee camp. She roused herself from her comfortable but empty life to make the distress of the refugees her own concern. Her leap from joylessness to fulfillment was striking.

Logotherapy helps patients write a new scenario. Making them feel and act as if they were in a period of scarcity, requires them to focus attention on a task, a goal, an answer to the question, "What for?" The question is not: to have or not to have, but: to be or not to be. The search for gain is replaced by search for meaning.

The old, paralyzed, and lonely man, for instance (case no. 24) was close to despair. He overcame despair as soon as his "inner scenario" changed, and he saw himself as an important example for others. Suddenly he realized a task—help others in situations of despair. He was able to see something meaningful he could do, or in this case, *not* do—commit suicide.

I remember another patient, an old woman in deep despair. She was a war widow, hardened by the war—and postwar years, worn out and bitter. The cause of her grief was not her war sufferings but the sum of 400,000 marks which she had saved in years of stringent self-sacrifices. She had worked in a laundry by day and taken in ironing at night to make sure she and her son would be well off later on. Her work left little time for the child but her desire for affluence kept her from slowing down her feverish work schedule. Her son, left to his own devices, got into the streets and began to steal. This made his mother work even harder to make financial amends for his thefts. After the school years, finished with poor grades, the young man lost job after job because he was unreliable and dishonest. He finally gave up looking for work altogether while his mother, burdened by worries, sought escape in more work. Now her son was in prison and the old woman was disinheriting him, leaving the 400,000 marks, the fruit of her labor, to an animal shelter. "That's what I lived and sweated for all these years," she moaned, "all for nothing."

This case is both a tragedy and a testimony to the dangers of the search for material gain at the expense of meaning. A "gain" of 400,000 marks for a mother who neglected her child, a lost human being as the price for scraping together a meaningless inheritance!

My case histories usually end with at least a therapeutic program to help the client see a glimmer of meaning. It is difficult to see a glimmer in this case except perhaps the meaning of a lesson that gain as such is dead unless life is breathed into it by meaning. Suffering often leaves us without hope. We feel helpless in the face of an unavoidable situation—the death of a close person, incurable illness, or unjust Fate. What causes deep despair is the apparent meaninglessness of the situation and our own helplessness. But meaning can be found behind every suffering, and every crisis offers a chance—at least the chance for a new and healthier attitude.

CONCLUSION

I often get requests for logotherapeutic techniques. I myself wished for a methodology when I started to use logotherapy. Now I know that a standardized guide would be more hindrance than help.

Every patient is different, none can be classified, even symptoms are clearly systematized only in textbooks. Only when we disregard the specifically human dimension of the spirit can we lump individuals into types to be treated by method A, B, or C. When we consider the human spirit, the therapist speaks to the client as one person to another—and there is no fixed method.

Modern psychotherapy works without a booklet of instruction. It does not see the patient as a machine to be repaired by a "psychomechanic." The assumption of human freedom within the patient requires the therapist to improvise. What is needed is understanding. This is especially true for logotherapy.

Therapists, by their methods, produce effects but seldom experience them. They can get patients to produce catathymic daydreams but the therapists do not see the images. They merely hear descriptions from patients. Therapists use autogenic training to produce feelings of calm or heaviness, but don't feel calm or heavy themselves. They get patients to remember the past but don't think about their own past because they are busy evaluating patients' memories. Methods place therapists outside the effects they produce and direct.

Logotherapy is more than a method. It is a healthy way of living that can be used in therapy if it is actually lived: first by the therapist, then—with the help of the therapist—by the patient. Which means: If you don't live logotherapy you cannot use it in healing.

This is one reason logotherapeutic practice is not primarily concerned with making profits. High value priority is meaning, helping people—not material gain. Patients who can be helped in two or three counseling sessions, are not asked to come to 50: this would only increase hyperreflection on their problems. Patients who need individual counseling are not asked to join a group if this would weaken their independent search for meaning.

Living the principles of logotherapy means offering part of yourself so a part of another person can live a healthier life.

BIBLIOGRAPHY OF VIKTOR FRANKL'S MAJOR WORKS IN ENGLISH

Most of the literature about logotherapy is available in the Viktor E. Frankl Library and Memorabilia, Graduate Theological Union, 2465 Le Conte, Berkeley, CA 94709.

BOOKS

Frankl, Viktor E., *The Doctor and the Soul: From Psychotherapy to Logotherapy.* New York, Alfred A. Knopf, Inc.; second, expanded edition, 1965; paperback edition, New York, Vintage Books, 1977.

Frankl, Viktor E., *Man's Search for Meaning: An Introduction to Logotherapy.* Preface by Gordon W. Allport. Boston, Beacon Press, 1959; paperback edition, New York, Pocket Books, 1985.

Frankl, Viktor E., *Psychotherapy and Existentialism: Selected Papers on Logotherapy.* New York, Washington Square Press, 1985.

Frankl, Viktor E., *The Will to Meaning: Foundations and Applications of Logotherapy.* New York and Cleveland, The World Publishing Company, 1969; paperback edition, New York, New American Library, 1981.

Frankl, Viktor E., *The Unconscious God: Psychotherapy and Theology.* New York, Simon and Schuster, 1985.

Frankl, Viktor E., *The Unheard Cry for Meaning: Psychotherapy and Humanism.* New York, Simon and Schuster, 1985.

Frankl, Viktor E., *Synchronization in Buchenwald,* a play, offset, $5.00. Available at the Institute of Logotherapy, 2000 Dwight Way, Berkeley, CA 94704.

CHAPTERS IN BOOKS

Frankl, Viktor E., Contributions to *Critical Incidents in Psychotherapy*, S. W. Standal and R. J. Corsini, eds. Englewood Cliffs, Prentice-Hall, 1959.

Frankl, Viktor E., "Logotherapy and the Collective Neuroses," in *Progress in Psychotherapy*, J. H. Masserman and J. L. Moreno, eds., New York, Grune & Stratton, 1959.

Frankl, Viktor E., "The Philosophical Foundations of Logotherapy" (paper read before the first Lexington Conference on Phenomenology on April 4, 1963), in *Phenomonology: Pure and Applied*, Erwin Straus, ed. Pittsburgh, Duquesne University Press, 1964.

Frankl, Viktor E., "Fragments from the Logotherapeutic Treatment of Four Cases. With an Introduction and Epilogue by G. Kaczanowski," in *Modern Psychotherapeutic Practices: Innovations in Technique*, Arthur Burton, ed. Palo Alto, Science and Behavior Books, 1965.

Frankl, Viktor E., "The Will to Meaning," in *Are You Nobody?* Richmond, Virginia, John Knox Press, 1966.

Frankl, Viktor E., "Accepting Responsibility" and "Overcoming Circumstances," in *Man's Search for a Meaningful Faith: Selected Readings*, Judith Weidmann, ed. Nashville, Graded Press, 1967.

Frankl, Viktor E. "Comment on Vatican II's Pastoral Constitution on the Church in the Modern World," in *World*. Chicago, Catholic Action Federations, 1967.

Frankl, Viktor E., "Paradoxical Intention: A Logotherapeutic Technique," in *Active Psychotherapy*, Harold Greenwald, ed. New York, Atherton Press, 1967.

Frankl, Viktor E., "The Significance of Meaning for Health," in *Religion and Medicine: Essays on Meaning, Values and Health*, David Belgum, ed. Ames, Iowa, The Iowa State University Press, 1967.

Frankl, Viktor E., "The Task of Education in an Age of Meaninglessness," in *New Prospects for the Small Liberal Arts College*, Sidney S. Letter, ed. New York, Teachers College Press, 1968.

Frankl, Viktor E., "Self-Transcendence as a Human Phenomenon," in *Readings in Humanistic Psychology*, Anthony J. Sutich and Miles A. Vich, eds. New York, The Free Press, 1969.

Frankl, Viktor E., "Beyond Self-Actualization and Self-Expression," in *Perspectives on the Group Process: A Foundation for Counseling with Groups*, C. Gratton Kemp, ed. Boston, Houghton Mifflin Company, 1970.

Frankl, Viktor E., "Logotherapy," in *Psychopathology Today: Experimentation, Theory and Research*, William S. Sahakian, ed. Itasca, Illinois, F. E. Peacock Publishers, 1970.

Frankl, Viktor E., "Reductionism and Nihilism," in *Beyond Reductionism: New Perspectives in the Life Sciences* (The Alpbach Symposium, 1968), Arthur Koestler and J. R. Smythies, eds. New York, Macmillan, 1970.

Frankl, Viktor E., "Universities and the Quest for Peace," in *Report of the First World Conference on the Role of the University in the Quest for Peace.* Binghamton, New York, State University of New York, 1970.

Frankl, Viktor E., "What Is Meant by Meaning?" in *Values in an Age of Confrontation,* Jeremiah W. Canning, ed. Columbus, Ohio, Charles E. Merrill Publishing Company, 1970.

Frankl, Viktor E., "Dynamics, Existence and Values" and "The Concept of Man in Logotherapy," in *Personality Theory: A Source Book,* Harold J. Vetter and Barry D. Smith, eds. New York, Appleton-Century-Crofts, 1971.

Frankl, Viktor E., "Youth in Search of Meaning," in *Students Search of Meaning,* James Edward Doty, ed. Kansas City, Missouri, The Lowell Press, 1971.

Frankl, Viktor E., "Address before the Third Annual Meeting of the Academy of Religion and Mental Health," in *Discovering Man in Psychology: A Humanistic Approach,* Frank T. Severin, ed. New York, McGraw-Hill, Inc. 1973.

Frankl, Viktor E., "Beyond Pluralism and Determinism," in *Unity Through Diversity: A Festschrift for Ludwig van Bertalanffy,* William Ray and Nicholas D. Rizzo, eds. New York, Gordon and Breach, 1973.

Frankl, Viktor E., "Meaninglessness: A Challenge to Psychologists," in *Theories of Psychopathology and Personality,* Theodore Millon, ed. Philadelphia, W. B. Saunders Company, 1973.

Frankl, Viktor E., "Encounter: The Concept and Its Vulgarization," in *Psychotherapy and Behavior Change 1973,* Hans H. Strupp et al., eds. Chicago, Aldine Publishing Company, 1974.

Frankl, Viktor E., "Paradoxical Intention and Dereflection: Two Logotherapeutic Techniques," in *New Dimensions in Psychiatry: A World View,* Silvano Arieti, ed. New York, John Wiley & Sons, Inc., 1975.

Frankl, Viktor E., "Logotherapy," in *Encyclopaedic Handbook of Medical Psychology,* Stephen Krauss, ed. London and Boston, Butterworth, 1976.

Frankl, Viktor E., "Man's Search for Ultimate Meaning," in *On the Way to Self-Knowledge,* Jacob Needleman, ed. New York, Alfred A. Knopf, Inc., 1976.

Frankl, Viktor E., "The Depersonalization of Sex," in *Humanistic Psychology: A Source Book,* I. David Welch, George A Tate and Fred Richards, eds, Buffalo, New York, Prometheus Books, 1978.

Frankl, Viktor E., "Meaninglessness: A Challenge to Psychiatry," in *Value and Values in Evolution,* Edward A. Maziarz, ed. New York, Gordon and Breach, 1979.

Frankl, Viktor E., "Logotherapy," in *The Psychotherapy Handbook,* Richie Herink, ed. New York, New American Library, 1980.

Frankl, Viktor E., "Opening Address to the First World Congress of Logotherapy: Logotherapy on its Way to Degurufication," in *Analecta Frankliana: The Proceedings of the First World Congress of Logotherapy [1980],* Sandra A. Wawrytko, ed. Berkeley, Institute of Logotherapy Press, 1982.

Frankl, Viktor E., "Logotherapy," in *Encyclopedia of Psychology,* Edited by Raymond J. Corsini, Volume 2. New York, John Wiley, 1984.

Frankl, Viktor E., "Paradoxical Intention," in *Promoting Change Through Paradoxical Therapy,* Gerald R. Weeks, ed. Homewood, Illinois, Dow Jones-Irwin, 1985.

Frankl, Viktor E., "Logos, Paradox, and the Search of Meaning, in *Cognition and Psychotherapy,* Edited by Michael J. Mahoney and Arthur Freeman. Plenum Press, New York, 1985.

ARTICLES

Frankl, Viktor E., "The Pleasure Principle and Sexual Neurosis." *International Journal of Sexology,* 5 (1952), 128-30.

Frankl, Viktor E., "Logos and Existence in Psychotherapy." *American Journal of Psychotherapy,* VII (1959), 8-15.

Frankl, Viktor E., "Group Psychotherapeutic Experiences in a Concentration Camp," (paper read before the second International Congress of Psychotherapy, Leiden, Netherlands, Sept. 8, 1951). *Group Psychotherapy,* VII (1954), 81-90.

Frankl, Viktor E., "The Concept of Man in Psychotherapy" (paper read before the Royal Society of Medicine, Section of Psychiatry, London, England, June 15, 1954). *Pastoral Psychology,* VI (1955), 16-26.

Frankl, Viktor E., "From Psychotherapy to Logotherapy." *Pastoral Psychology,* VII (1956), 56-60.

Frankl, Viktor E., "Guest Editorial." *Academy Reporter,* III, No. 5 (May 1958), 1-4.

Frankl, Viktor E.,"On Logotherapy and Existential Analysis" (paper read before the Association for the Advancement of Psychoanalysis, New York, April 17, 1957). *American Journal of Psychoanalysis,* XVIII (1958), 28-37.

Frankl, Viktor E., "The Search for Meaning." *Saturday Review* (Sept. 13, 1958).

Frankl, Viktor E., "The Will to Meaning." *Journal of Pastoral Care,* XII (1958), 82-88.

Frankl, Viktor E., "The Spiritual Dimension in Existential Analysis and Logotherapy" (paper read before the Fourth International Congress of Psychotherapy, Barcelona, Sept. 5, 1958). *Journal of Individual Psychology,* XV (1959), 157-65.

Frankl, Viktor E., "Beyond Self-Actualization and Self-Expression" (paper read before the Conference on Existential Psychotherapy, Chicago, Dec. 13, 1959). *Journal of Existential Psychiatry,* I (1960), 5-20.

Frankl, Viktor E., "Paradoxical Intention: A Logotherapeutic Technique" (paper read before the American Association for the Advancement of Psychotherapy, New York, Feb. 26, 1960). *American Journal of Psychotherapy,* XIV (1960), 520-35.

Frankl, Viktor E., "Dynamics, Existence and Values." *Journal of Existential Psychiatry,* II (1961). 5-16.

Frankl, Viktor E., "Logotherapy and the Challenge of Suffering" (paper read before the American Conference on Existential Psychotherapy, New York, Feb. 27, 1960). *Review of Existential Psychology and Psychiatry,* I (1961), 3-7.

Frankl, Viktor E., "Psychotherapy and Philosophy." *Philosophy Today,* V (1961), 59-64.

Frankl, Viktor E., "Religion and Existential Psychotherapy." *Gordon Review,* VI (1961), 2-10.

Frankl, Viktor E., "Basic Concepts of Logotherapy," *Journal of Existential Psychiatry,* III (1962), 111-18.

Frankl, Viktor E., "Logotherapy and the Challenge of Suffering." *Pastoral Psychology,* XIII (1962), 25-28.

Frankl, Viktor E., "Psychiatry and Man's Quest for Meaning." *Journal of Religion and Health,* I (1962), 93-103.

Frankl, Viktor E., "The Will to Meaning." *Living Church,* CXLIV (June 24, 1962), 8-14.

Frankl, Viktor E., "Angel as Much as Beast: Man Transcends Himself." *Unitarian Universalist Register-Leader,* CXLIV (Feb. 1963), 8-9.

Frankl, Viktor E., "Existential Dynamics and Neurotic Escapism" (paper read before the Conference on Existential Psychiatry, Toronto, May 6, 1962). *Journal of Existential Psychiatry,* IV (1963), 27-42.

Frankl, Viktor E., "Existential Escapism." *Motive*, XXIV (Jan.-Feb. 1964), 11-14.

Frankl, Viktor E., "In Steady Search for Meaning." *Liberal Dimension*, II, No. 2 (1964), 3-8.

Frankl, Viktor E., "The Will to Meaning" (paper read before the Conference on Phenomenology, Lexington, April 4, 1963). *Christian Century*, LXXI (April 22, 1964), 515-17.

Frankl, Viktor E., "How a Sense of a Task in Life Can Help You Over the Bumps." *The National Observer*, July 12, 1964, 22.

Frankl, Viktor E., "The Concept of Man in Logotherapy" (175th Anniversary Lecture, Georgetown University, Washington, D. C., February 27, 1964). *Journal of Existentialism*, VI (1965), 53-58.

Frankl, Viktor E., "Logotherapy—a New Psychology of Man." *The Gadfly*, Volume 17, Issue 1, December, 1965—January, 1966.

Frankl, Viktor E., "Logotherapy and Existential Analysis: A Reveiw" (paper read before the Symposium on Logotherapy, 6th International Congress of Psychotherapy, London, August 26, 1964). *American Journal of Psychotherapy*, XX (1966), 252-60.

Frankl, Viktor E., "Self-Transcendence As a Human Phenomenon." *Journal of Humanistic Psychology*, VI, No. 2 (Fall 1966) 97-106.

Frankl, Viktor E., "Time and Responsibility." *Existential Psychiatry*, I (1966), 361-66.

Frankl, Viktor E., "What Is Meant by Meaning?" *Journal of Existentialism*, VII, No. 25 (Fall 1966), 21-28.

Frankl, Viktor E., "Logotherapy."*The Israel Annals of Psychiatry and Related Disciplines*, VII (1967), 142-55.

Frankl, Viktor E., "Logotherapy and Existentialism." *Psychotherapy: Theory, Research and Practice*, IV, No. 3 (Aug. 1967), 138-42.

Frankl, Viktor E., "What is a Man?" *Life Association News*, LXII, No. 9 (Sept. 1967), 151-57.

Frankl, Viktor E., "Experiences in A Concentration Camp." *Jewish Heritage*, XI (1968), 5-7.

Frankl, Viktor E., "The Search for Meaning" (Abstract from a series of lectures given at the Brandeis Institute in California). *Jewish Heritage*, XI (1968), 8-11.

Frankl, Viktor E., "The Cosmos and the Mind. (How Far Can We Go?) A Dialogue with Geoffrey Frost." *Pace*, V, No. 8 (Aug. 1969), 34-39.

Frankl, Viktor E., "Eternity Is the Here and Now." *Pace*, V, No. 4 (April 1969), 2.

Frankl, Viktor E., "Youth in Search for Meaning" (Third Paul Dana Bartlett Memorial Lecture). *The Baker World* (The Baker University Newsletter), I, No. 4 (Jan. 1969), 2-5.

Frankl, Viktor E., "Entering the Human Dimension." *Attitude,* I (1970), 2-6.

Frankl, Viktor E., "Forerunner of Existential Psychiatry." *Journal of Individual Psychology,* XXVI (1970), 12.

Frankl, Viktor E., "Determinism and Humanism." *Humanitas* [*Journal of the Institute of Man*], VII (1971), 23-36.

Frankl, Viktor E., "Existential Escapism." *Omega,* Vol. 2, No. 4, November, 1971, 307-311.

Frankl, Viktor E., "The Feeling of Meaninglessness: A Challenge to Psychotherapy." *The American Journal of Psychoanalysis,* XXXII, No. 1 (1972), 85-89.

Frankl, Viktor E., "Man in Search of Meaning." *Widening Horizons* (Rockford College), Vol. 8, No. 5 (Aug. 1972).

Frankl, Viktor E., "Encounter: The Concept and Its Vulgarization." *The Journal of the American Academy of Psychoanalysis,* I, No. 1 (1973), 73-83.

Frankl, Viktor E., "The Depersonalization of Sex." *Synthesis* [*The Realization of the Self*], I (Spring 1974), 7-11.

Frankl, Viktor E., "Paradoxial Intention and Dereflection." *Psychotherapy: Theory, Research and Practice,* XII, No. 3 (Fall 1975), 226-37.

Frankl, Viktor E., "A Psychiatrist Looks at Love." *Uniquest* (The First Unitarian Church of Berkeley), 5, 1975, 6-9.

Frankl, Viktor E., "Some Thoughts on the Painful Wisdom." *Uniquest* (The First Unitarian Church of Berkeley), 6, 1976, 3.

Frankl, Viktor E., "Survival—for What? *Uniquest* (The First Unitarian Church of Berkeley), 6, 1976, 38.

Frankl, Viktor E., "Logotherapy." *The International Forum for Logotherapy,* Volume 1, Number 1, Winter 1978—Spring 1979, 22-23.

Frankl, Viktor E., "Endogenous Depression and Noogenic Neurosis" *The International Forum for Logotherapy,* Volume 2, Number 2, Summer-Fall 1979, 38-40.

Frankl, Viktor E., "Psychotherapy on its Way to Rehumanization." *The International Forum for Logotherapy,* Volume 3, Number 2, Fall 1980, 3-9.

Frankl, Viktor E., "The Future of Logotherapy." *The International Forum for Logotherapy,* Volume 4, Number 2, Fall/Winter 1981, 71-78.

Frankl, Viktor E., "The Meaning Crisis in the First World and Hunger in the Third World." *The International Forum for Logotherapy,* Volume 7, Number 1, Spring/Summer 1984, 5-7.